POSITIVE SELLING

In the same series

Business Letters
The Right Way To Write Your Own C.V.
The Right Way To Apply For A Job

All uniform with this book

POSITIVE SELLING

by

Richard Moss

PAPERFRONTS
ELLIOT RIGHT WAY BOOKS
KINGSWOOD, SURREY, U.K.

Typeset in 10/11½pt Times
by County Typesetters, Margate, Kent.

Made and Printed in Great Britain by
Richard Clay Ltd., Bungay, Suffolk.

CONTENTS

1

THE DEATH OF A
SALES PITCH

Whether you're selling over the counter, to the general public or out of a hatchback to the trade, learning a sales pitch won't fill the food cupboard any more. Yet it's still the technique most fledgling salespeople are taught before they are thrust eyeball to eyeball with the foe!

Having the patter might have worked twenty-five years ago, but even then, professional salesmen who had learned their lines to perfection were bedevilled by customers who kept forgetting theirs!

Today's buyers have to be understood rather than pitched at. People are more sophisticated, generally better educated and more intelligent than before. It makes no difference what is being bought or sold, the old canned sales pitch has withered and died. We need to throw away the script and work with two other concepts.

People buy for their own reasons
The first concept is: "People buy for their own reasons, not for ours." It doesn't matter how stupid their reasons may seem to us.

My wife needs a new car. She has set her heart on a Citroën 2CV Charleston with two-tone bodywork in black and mauve. She has used all her persuasive powers for the past three months convincing me that her old car would never pass its roadworthiness test and has conditionally closed me very skilfully with: "All right, clever clogs, if it passes, I won't point to another Charleston again. But if it fails, you must promise to buy me that one down at Fred's Garage."

I know Fred is in on it; a car like hers doesn't just fall apart after ten years, but he says it has. I go for a second opinion. But it's no good, Fred must have spiked it.

Her face almost splits in two she's so happy. So I dust off my cheque book, we dump the terrors on mum-in-law and go to buy a motor car.

Fred was out, so we landed Dennis; his thin waxed moustache quivered when my wife informed him we had come to buy a car.

"Is it just for the two of you?" he asked.

"No it's for me," chirped my wife puffing out her chest a little as she smiled the answer.

"No madam, what I mean is have you got any children?" His smile didn't reach his eyes as he cocked his head to one side, folded his arms and silently demanded an answer.

"Uh oh" thought I, "he's been to the school of car salesmen, we're about to get his pitch."

"Yes," said mum. "Why?"

"Is it a big family?" They taught him to ask that next.

"Well, the boy just about reaches up to my shoulders but the girls are much smaller." I probably wouldn't have noticed the trace of irritation in her voice, either, if I hadn't been the target of it so many times in the past.

He ploughed on. "So. There are five of you. What you need is the new Nisda estate with triple kiddies' seat-belts in the rear, which makes it the safest estate car in the country today. In fact statistics have shown..."

He was backing away towards the Nisda, facing us with arms stretched out in front of him, and I must say I'd taken a step or two with him before her little hiss stopped us both. The difference was that I knew he was in trouble.

"No Dennis. I want the Charleston. There. The black and

mauve one. With the mudflaps." Now her smile fell short of her feelings. She stood her ground.

"But this Nisda will be far more suitable, you can get all the kids strapped safely into the back seat and have plenty of room for your shopping." His sales course must have majored on selling safety and you can bet money it was sponsored by Nisda.

"It's not what I want," said my wife, her sweet temper beginning to glow. "It's too big, I won't be able to get it in the drive...."

"Oh that's no problem." He interrupted her, "the power steering will help you with that." He wasn't listening, "and just think of your little ones' safety." Back to the sales course.

"... and it isn't purple and black."

Being cooped up with the kids all day, every moment of concentration tuned into their welfare, this purchase was to be her little extravagance not theirs. Besides I have a big car, for heavy shopping trips and family outings.

"Now, now, surely madam isn't going to put a colour scheme before the safety of her children is she?" It's funny how you can't keep a smug look on your face when you're trying to duck a well swung handbag.

We bought the Citroën from Fred, who mopped up his commission, while Dennis mopped up his bloody nose in a quiet corner of the showroom.

My wife had bought that car for her own personal reasons and no matter how misguided Dennis thought those reasons to be, he wasn't going to get her money – well, my money – unless he tuned in to them. His pitch may have been as polished as the bottom of a bricklayer's tea mug, but as a sales technique it was useless!

Take Mr. and Mrs. Window-Customer, who come into the showroom wanting replacement windows with a mahogany surround, "because it will match the wooden doors on the kitchen."

You don't like hardwood windows, you feel they should

ignore the mahogany and have UPVC. You think you're going to save them maintenance because UPVC doesn't need varnishing. You explain that mahogany is very expensive, and it has to have a metal frame, which will cause condensation. You try hard to sell them UPVC on its value and ease of maintenance.

They go away to think about what you said. And the next day they give their money to the joiner down the road, who sold them mahogany windows that match the doors on their kitchen.

Mrs. Customer may want a microwave because all the ladies at her coffee morning are talking about their new microwaves and she can't join in the conversation. Sell her plenty to talk about.

Mr. Customer may want a new caravan to silence his greasy brother-in-law who has recently bought one and has talked of nothing else for the last two months. Sell him something to take greasy's breath away.

They may have just set up home, be short of cash, and be in desperate need of a bed to sleep on. Sell them pocket sprung hire purchase.

They may love driving like the wind with the breeze in their hair. Sell them twin carburettors and overhead camshafts, horsepower and racing suspension. And the fastest looking soft-top on your lot.

They may love touring round the countryside in comfort and style. Sell them Connelly hide seats and spacious interiors, quadrophonic radio and a soft ride. And the quietest, smoothest sedan you have.

They may be five foot tall and dumpy. If you want repeat business, avoid chest freezers!

The daftest reason I ever bought from someone was because we shared a common interest.

As an electrical retailer, it was never really important whose electrical appliance I sold. They are all very much of a muchness; the ovens cook and the fridges cool things. The

If you want repeat business, avoid chest freezers!

profit margins are close enough and the selling prices differ by pounds rather than fivers. So I sold what I wanted to.

The chap had a busload of competitors, all of whose ranges were riddled with the same features and benefits that his range was. One day he happened to mention his weekend outing to Silverstone to watch the Grand Prix. For an hour we talked motor racing and he went away with an order.

Now, every time he comes in I look forward to a good chin-wag about championship contenders, engines, racing drivers and who he thinks will win the next race – we rarely talk about his product, unless there's something new. I buy his product like a freshly imported harem let loose in Harrods.

People buy on emotion
The second concept is: "People buy on emotion and justify afterwards with facts."

Nine times out of ten, that emotion will revolve round the effect our purchase has on other people. This relates to professional buyers working for multi-nationals just as much as it does to Mrs. Housewife coming in to buy our products. She just spent £950 on new curtains. Why? Is it to keep the light out? Is it to stop draughts? Is it because the fabric is guaranteed not to fade? Or is it, perhaps, because mother-in-law is visiting next month and she wants to impress the old dear!

Similarly a buying manager, having negotiated with several manufacturers for hi-tech components to keep his company's production line singing, finds a new make that will save his company £50,000 per year. Does he buy it?

He knows that his Managing Director is a personal friend of their regular supplier. He also knows that the present deal was set up by his M.D. before he joined the company.

The new product is clearly best for the job. But he decides not to stick his neck out in case he upsets his M.D. and loses the promotion he's been working so hard for.

You are the salesman he is about to turn down. What can you do? Take the buyer and his M.D. out to lunch, or for a round of golf. Make a friend of the M.D. and a sale to the buyer. Sell him the thought that £50,000 saved will bring that promotion closer.

A builder's merchant buys the brand of central heating boiler whose service department is most efficient. The others could have 10% more insulation, burn their fuel more efficiently, be kinder on the environment and come in colours he never dreamed of, but he buys peace from irate customers and a safeguard for his reputation.

Even when it comes to buying our most major purchase, a house and home, emotion comes to the fore.

One very good friend of mine had to move with his job. He'd cut the short-list down to two houses that he would like to buy, with the off-chance of a third house which he could modernise. He wasn't that keen on renovating the old house, preferring to move straight into a finished home.

To keep his option open he made a low offer on the house needing renovation. When the offer was accepted he went round once more to look the place over. He was unimpressed until he got talking to an old man who was tending his orchard next door. At the end of their chat he'd decided to buy the old house.

When I asked him why, he said he found it hard to explain but the old chap had made him feel good about the place and really he'd bought the house on the strength of that feeling.

He justified it afterwards with the facts that he could extend the house and model it to his individual tastes, that a local government grant was available to finance some of the work, that it would probably be worth much more when he'd finished than it was now. But really he bought it because he was charmed by his neighbour.

Just before we leave "the death of a sales pitch," I'd like to add that although the scripted pitch is no longer viable it does no harm to have practised answers to the common questions which crop up time and again.

People buy for their own reasons not ours. People buy on emotion, so let's sell to that emotion, those feelings, and justify afterwards with facts.

2

SELF-IMPROVEMENT

Have you been to many sales training seminars?

Me too. Did you notice that most sales training philosophy is broken down into two sections: one is product knowledge, the second is training in sales skills. But that's not enough.

There is a third section, probably the most important section, and that is training in the development of the individual. By this I mean our self-confidence, our drive, our projection, our enthusiasm, our powers of persuasion.

Working on the belief that perfect folk are very rare, all these personal attributes can be improved in every one of us, so let's look at self-improvement.

Any discussion on self-improvement will be riddled with tenuous theories. Some of it you'll use, other parts you'll really laugh at. Before you do either, open your mind, suck the ideas in, and risk a trial period. You've "now't to lose" and the gains can be incredible. Here are a few ideas.

Be yourself
Idea number one starts with the words, "Be yourself." You have no choice anyway. You'll never change your basic character but you can learn, and to some degree you can train yourself, to be more successful.

A few years ago two of the most used buzz words in sales training were "role modelling." It meant that you found someone successful, and you copied them. It never worked.

Fledgling sellers often found that their "successful" models weren't all they were cracked up to be.

No matter how hard the newcomer tried, and no matter how skilled their model salesman was; prising pensions out of septuagenarians' fingers, in exchange for membership of the 18/30s club, was just too much for the trainee to swallow. Role modelling was always doomed to failure.

Which brings me to the question: "What is a success?" I don't know. But I've a fair idea where failure starts. It starts when you try to please everybody. You end up by pleasing nobody and especially you end up by not pleasing you. Then anything you do stops being enjoyable.

You try to conform to everyone else's opinion of what you should be, and that diminishes your uniqueness, which is the most valuable thing you've got in the first place.

People buy people before products. If you're trying to sell them something that you are not, those people will suss you out. You are unique. Sell yourself to you. Then sell yourself to others.

Self-confidence

There isn't a person alive who doesn't fear rejection by his fellows. As salespeople, this fear is a luxury we just cannot afford. It saps self-confidence. We have to live on confidence. Confidence in ourselves, in our suppliers and in the products we sell.

The biggest single cause of failure to close a sale is because our confidence falters under pressure.

We've completed our sales presentation, they're quiet and unsmiling and we are dying to ask for their order. But we don't. They look at us, wondering what to do. We look at them and smile nervously. They say something like – "We want to go and think about it."

And a huge rush of relief spews out of us in the form of "Fine.. yes... I think that's what you should do. Do you want any more brochures? Can I check some more prices for you? Would it help if I could arrange for a manufacturer's demonstration?" And on we go, blah ... blah ... blah ... blah ... blah.

The pressure of the sale turns us into a babbling amateur. The best way to combat pressure is to practise.

Practice

The sportsman who was undoubtedly best at what he did was Mohammed Ali (also known as Cassius Clay, the former world heavyweight champion boxer). He practised building self belief every moment he could. He not only told himself he was "the greatest", he told his opponents and anybody else within earshot as well. Some folk found that a bit tedious but its effect was knock-out!

When was the last time you told yourself you were the greatest? You need to. No-one else will. Like Ali, there's no-one else for you to model yourself on. You are the only one of you in the world, so tell yourself how good you are, and practise.

Actually the first time I heard this idea put forward I was no'but a lad. All grease and acne. The lecturer spoke thus:- "and every morning, when you rise, go first to the bathroom."

Well after three halves of shandy the previous night, where else should I go?

"Stand fore square to the mirror," he said, "and issue forth the words, "I am absolutely fantastic." Do not falter from your task, 'til it is fully believed inside your head."

He had a queer way of talking. I didn't go for his walk much either. Anyhow I tried it. Once.

Up to the mirror, shining and spotty – "I am truly fantastic!" My sister was watching; she fell apart laughing, wet the carpet and we both got grounded for a week. I speak more quietly now.

In the early days I used to practise my sales presentations

"I am truly fantastic!"

with a colleague before seeing a client.

Sometimes it was as useful as second-hand loo roll. But it was uncanny how often an objection had cropped up in practice that was repeated in the real thing, and I was ready for it. It helped my confidence no end and the more it worked, the more I practised.

Give to others

Practise giving little compliments to other people. It makes them feel good, and that makes you feel good. If you don't feel good about yourself, you won't do a good job of selling. You won't do a good job of anything if it comes to that!

Whether it's your customers or your colleagues, your family or your employers, if you can get them feeling good about you, you've cracked it.

One salesman was trying to sell me a product I hadn't been convinced about. He answered one of my objections with

"That's a very good question."

It was like a bolt out of the blue. I took it as a great compliment and the thoughts running through my mind were on the lines of . . .

"Hey, he said that was a good question – Aren't I clever – I like this bloke – He's right, it was a good question."

So much so that I'd stopped listening to what he was actually saying and when he concluded with: "Don't you agree?" I just had to say "Yes."

I hadn't a clue what I was agreeing to but I couldn't disagree, not when he'd said such nice things. It wouldn't have been cricket, what!

Practise smiling. That makes you feel good. The better you feel, the better you'll perform. It also makes the people you smile at feel good; people who feel good are more receptive.

I learnt the power of this fact early one Monday morning, I had no sooner sat down at my desk when a pair of salespeople breezed into the office. One old hand, one newcomer. The newcomer was wearing a puce green tie that almost inspired my hastily consumed breakfast to come out in sympathy.

The old hand was wearing a smile that lit up the whole morning. She made us feel good. We had known them about three minutes but that smile had us joking with each other after four minutes and talking business in five.

When she took her trainee away the mood in our office was buzzing. Both my colleague and I were hopelessly in love and, short of spending money on her, would have done anything she wanted.

Then he slouched in. Face as long as a wet Wednesday, voice as flat as sour cream. Clothes as dingy as a well used dust-bag. He was from a credit card company. And he was boring.

We hadn't used our card machine since Muffin was a mule. This machine had a number, and he knew what it was. He had written to us several times. And could he have it back?

No he damned well couldn't! We had been aglow from the

radiance of a fabulous smile, now we shivered in the draught of a scowl and a whimper. He made us feel bad. We were as receptive to his requests as Stalin was to capitalism.

Do what you're good at

Your nine-year-old's teacher calls you in. Sir is a soccer freak and sonny boy has got less dribbling ability than a parking meter. So he's no Pele but just look at the way he has taken to knitting.

If he wants to knit let him knit. When he's producing pullovers to perfection he'll have built up the confidence to go on to other things.

Force him into a goal mouth scramble, yell in his ear that he's hopeless at it, and his potential confidence level will be lower than the sea-bed. This happens with sickening regularity. He also serves who provides the team with socks.

What I am trying to say is: "If you want to be a success at what you're doing, do what you're good at."

There are at least two master salesmen I know, and I mean master salesmen. Both very flamboyant, creative and great persuaders, salesmen extraordinaire.

Both men progressed to owning their own businesses. Then both made the same mistake. They stopped selling and started administering. After all, they thought, that's what bosses do. They were master salesmen, but on a scale 1 to 10 scored 0 as administrators. Both businesses went bust.

If you are good at selling, sell. Hire someone else to fiddle with paper, to crunch numbers and if necessary to manage you. Do what you are good at.

Do what you enjoy doing

I have known Stuart for eight years, during which time I have come to respect him as one of the finest craftsmen I have ever met. When I spoke to him that morning he was surveying yet another immaculately tiled floor and whistling merrily as he flashed me a smile.

"Stuart," said I, "don't you get fed up, tiling floors and walls day after day, week in week out?"

He wouldn't have been so perplexed by my question if he'd seen me at home the week before. Half way across the utility room surrounded by broken tiles and up to my dentures in grout and matchsticks!

"No." He said, "I love it." His answer surprised me at first, I mean how can anyone love tiling? But, when I had thought about it, I came to realise that he had to love his work to be as good as he is. If he didn't love his work, the best he could hope to be, would be ... just good enough.

So, do what you enjoy, it's the only way you will end up being very good at anything.

Warts 'n' all

Don't be too surprised if you feel you've got the odd weakness. There are very few of us perfect folk left these days.

Too many courses on self-improvement concentrate on the fatuous art of wart removal. Let's take a tip from Oliver Cromwell. He had one of the most famous warty noses in history, but he was picking it long after King Charles's head had been picked out of the executioner's basket.

By all means face up to your weaknesses; it helps to know what they are. But don't waste a lifetime trying to improve on what you are bad at, or agonising over the fact that you see yourself as weak in some skill or other. Concentrate on your strengths as Cromwell did.

If you can't come to terms with the "clever" closes, like "Would you like to sign with the black pen, or the blue one?" or "Would you like delivery this month or next?" don't use them. Ask in your own way. If that is "Can I have the order?", use it.

Theorists and trainers all over the country may throw up their arms and scream about it being just the type of question that encourages a "No." So it is, but take a chance. It's your sale. Do it your way.

You may find, that when the question is easy to answer with a "No", it's just as easy to answer with a "Yes."

Get your brain on your side
There's been a lot said in recent years about getting your subconscious, or imagination, on your side. Training your subconscious to believe you are great will guide your actions and thoughts so that you live up to it.

There are so many ways that your subconscious can work for you. The best thing you can say about half the medicines our doctors dish out is that they won't do us any harm. They're placebos to make us believe we're getting well. People can imagine themselves into deep depressions and illness. Or they can imagine themselves to be successful.

I first got my subconscious to work effectively during school exams. I didn't pick up much at school, I mean, all the lessons were taken by teachers, but one of them got one thing right.

"When you first get your question paper," he said, "read all the questions before you start. Then do the easiest first. While you're doing that one you will find that your subconscious has been working on the other questions and when you read them through again, they'll seem much easier."

He was right. When I first read the question paper, six out of six questions were impossible. But after I had tackled the first one, that changed to: three passable, and three, "I hope he's in a good mood when he marks these", which saw me hover near the pass mark.

It is desire more than ability that determines success
Most successful people can be accused of having bags of "front". Total belief in themselves. They may be quite ordinary folk but their desire to be a "success" is so powerful that they become what they imagine themselves to be. It happens.

Some successful people I know like to write down, on little

cards to keep in their top pockets, or on placards to hang on their office walls, all kinds of maxims to help them build up this "front." My favourite is:

> Life's battles are not always won,
> By the stronger or faster man,
> But sooner or later the man who wins,
> Is the one who thinks he can.

To these successful people, it's just an effective form of practising.

So here we have it, how to build a successful career. Be yourself. Practise, to build self-confidence. Do what you enjoy. Do what you're good at. Ignore what you're bad at, let someone else do that. Make a concerted effort to convince your sub-conscious that you are superbly successful, so that it may help you to become so. Try hard to help others to become a success; you will reap what you sow. And most of all, want success. Anyone can succeed if they really try.

And finally, when you are selling, take any edge you can to help you finish first. Coming second in this game, doesn't earn the prize-money.

3

ATTITUDES – NEGATIVE
OR POSITIVE

A change in attitude can motivate an outstanding change in results.

If you're a pessimist, try and think of anyone you know of, who has achieved in life all that you would like to achieve. And shares your pessimistic attitude.

That should keep the "can't be done" mob busy for the next year or two, now let's concentrate on us optimists.

We have a lot to put up with. The vast majority of people in this country just love to spread bad news. And they travel the world to gather it.

Bad news is negative. Ignore it, search out the good news. Look for what is going right. Who is doing well. Study them and follow the positive route. You might find yourself out on your own. If so, great, there's less competition out there.

The destructive negatives
Criticism, condemnation and complaints are destructive negatives. The most common obstacle to an enthusiastic salesman, who wants to try something ambitious, is negative comment from someone he knows. It might be his parents, his colleagues, sometimes even his manager.

The next time someone tells you: "You can't do that, it's impossible. You're not qualified. You've never done it before."

Don't listen. Don't allow them to stop you, or make you feel bad. Instead find out why they are trying to put you off.

It's usually because your success would remove the justification they have for sitting on their backsides and not achieving anything.

Sometimes it is simply that they hold a negative opinion on the matter. Could even be someone else's opinion. They've never actually engaged their brains and thought about it.

Never confuse opinions with facts. Especially if they are the opinions of someone who is less successful than you are.

Take the conversation between the wizened old carpenter, Bert, and the young fresh kitchen salesman, Justin. Young fresh Justin has completed a stint studying kitchen design on a specially commissioned seminar followed by a day in the hands of your manufacturer. He is enthusiastic, excited and looking forward to getting to grips with his very first "SmartnSparklin" kitchen.

Monday morning, he skips in early, he can't wait to see the display units, which are being fitted in the showroom. But then he meets Bert.

"Gosh aren't they thoooper," grins Justin. "Did you ever see such craftsmanship?"

"Craftsmanship. Call this craftsmanship. They're not a patch on that German stuff we used to sell. Must be a lot cheaper. That's all I can say."

"Oh," thinks Justin, his buoyant mood slumping just a little. "No they're not cheaper, in fact we're going up-market. These are the best units made today."

"What does this sprout know?" ponders Bert, the grease on his bacon breakfast giving his mobile innards more gyp than usual. "Pah. Up-market, call this up-market, just look at the finish on this end panel. The Germans wouldn't stand for that."

"But it's meant to be like that, it's called semi-distressed. They said on the course that these...."

"Said on a course." Bert butted-in. "What course? What

do they know anyway? I've been fitting kitchens for over twenty years and the horror stories I can tell you."

And he does. Any confidence or enthusiasm Justin had for his job gets ground into the ash tray like one of Bert's dog ends. Funny how Bert can't realise that his future employment depends so much on the young man's positive attitude. Perhaps he's looking forward to a good old moan about how they made him redundant.

It goes the other way too. You have just sold a very big landscaping project. Your gardeners are going to be at the client's home for at least eight weeks. Planting rockeries, digging a garden pool, laying drives, laying out shrubberies, constructing dry stone walls, building a pergola. The lot!

The first thing that your workers like to do is to strike up a good relationship. It helps them, in case any snags occur while they're under the microscope of Mr. and Mrs. Fussy's eagle eye.

You send them off, with the joyous news that:- "She's all right. But just wait till you meet him. He's horrible, one of the worst blokes I've ever had to deal with."

You might feel you are just forewarning them but all of a sudden they are thinking – "Oh dear me, I don't relish the thought of going now, and I was so looking forward to it. I wonder if that's my bad back I can feel coming on."

You are just as guilty as Bert of pouring negative opinions down their shell-like ears. Mr. Fussy could just have been smarting that you have relieved him of so much money. In fact his ambition could have been to provide the workers' ultimate dream: a never emptying tea pot!

Paint positive pictures
Replace negative pictures in your mind with positive ones. It's a matter of asking yourself to think about how you can achieve your objectives, instead of jumping straight in with a dozen reasons why you can't.

The time a positive outlook is doubly important is when

sales are bad.

A string of: "Thanks for all the work you've done for us, but we've decided to buy from elsewhere" can sting the confidence into a semi-depressed state where every new enquiry is looked on as just another opportunity for rejection.

It's at times like this when the best solution is a positive look at the activity needed to determine better results. If it helps, imagine how someone you see as successful would react in your situation.

Associate with positive people

It is my belief that the vast majority of people in this country suffer from an excess of negative attitudes. This belief has its roots firmly bedded in all the experience I have had trying to motivate my staff to achieve results which they knew "just couldn't be done". They could give endless lists of reasons "why not"; while very few were able to suggest "how" such results could be achieved.

So, looking at it another way, most of the people whom we associate with in our daily dealings are going to give us a negative attitude.

It has also come to my notice that we all conform to our surroundings. We must ensure that we do not conform to the negative folk who cannot achieve success.

To prove the conforming rule, to yourself, think of the last time you rolled into the office at the start of one of *those* days.

It begins when you open the mail and find that two of your suppliers are taking you to court, three of your customers have written to say how dissatisfied they are with your company and you've received a note from the Tax authorities, informing you that they intend to do a full audit.

Ever had a day like that? That mood will be transformed by a good presentation with a genuine couple who are pleasant, jovial and buying.

But, you will be sent suicidal by the couple who are about

as lively as a pound of raw liver. No matter how hard you enthuse, how skilfully you present your wares, they give you no more response than a blank stare and a miserable face. They may still buy. But they leave you feeling flat.

You conform to the people who surround you. Surround yourself with positive people.

It's the best way to stand out from the mass, and you don't need to stand out far.

To earn twice, or three times the national average wage does not mean we have to be twice, or three times as good as average.

At the 1984 Olympics, Carl Lewis sprinted to three gold medals. He wasn't three times as fast as his rivals. He may have been a hundredth of a second better. Just a nose in front.

First place can pay ten times as much as second place. Keep your nose ahead. Also-rans get nothing at all.

Decide to form a positive opinion of your own. Communicate your opinions with enthusiasm. Avoid negative folk at all costs, do not allow them to dump their rubbishy opinions in your brain. Repel them with the strongest means at your disposal, but remember to wipe off the fingerprints.

Never be tempted to follow. Chances are you will be following a follower.

Enthusiasts do it while you're awake
The simplest ingredient to finishing a nose ahead is enthusiasm. Enthusiasm is an enormously powerful tool. People find it very difficult to nod off in the presence of someone who pours passion into his persuasive power.

Lack of enthusiasm is easily recognised by the frequency of sighs from both speaker and listener. Always assuming the listener's ears aren't full of the sound of his own snoring.

Catch them young
The other nasty thing about negative thinkers is they're always proved right. If they say they can't do it, they can't.

Somebody who has a positive view probably can. But not them.

I don't really believe people are born negative. That's hammered into them throughout childhood. Dad is up to his waist in non-drip emulsion and his five-year-old asks a perfectly reasonable question.

"Da-a-ad. Dad. DAD?"

"What?" Dad's painting the ceiling and a brushful of brilliant white has just rendezvoused with the hairs in his armpit.

"Can I do a bit Dad?" Asks sonny Jim, all inquisitiveness and innocence.

"No you can't!"

"Why not Dad? Oh go on Dad. Just a bit. That bit there, can I do that bit. Dad?" Sonny is smiling and wide open.

"No. I said no. You can't do it. You'll spoil it."

I don't know about you but when I was young I believed every last thing my parents told me. I didn't start to doubt them until I was eight.

I'd woken up early one morning for some pressing reason. When I brought this to the attention of my slumbering mum she asked me politely to return to my bed with: "Don't you know what time it is? It's 3 o'clock . . . it's the middle of the night, for goodness sake."

I believed her. To-the-letter. The next week that belief cost me dear. I gambled my pocket money, with the spotty creep next door. I knew, didn't I, that 3 o'clock was the middle of the night. Ha Ha, that clever little custard thought it was 12 o'clock.

I was really looking forward to taking his money off him and then. She changed her mind. All of a sudden the middle of the night was 12 o'clock and I was down a lucky bag, four liquorice chews, an iced lolly and two tubes of smarties, which was my idea of a masterly investment of capital in those days. It still would be but they don't make lucky bags like they used to.

So imagine our little chap whose dad has just told him he's a rubbish painter. He'll believe it, just as I did. How much better to give him some wall to paint and enough encouragement and time to see that he's doing it well.

If he's been a horror all week you can leave him a patch just beneath where you're loading the emulsion on with a roller. A few well aimed flicks and you'll get your own back without denting his confidence in any way!

If there's one thing worse than the pain of trying to clean dried Dulux off all those little hairs on the back of your forearm it's a good dollop of Apple White straight down the parting.

No! No! No! You Can't do this. Or that, or the other. Pests aren't born; they're conditioned from birth. "Pest", by the way, is an affectionate term to describe negative people. It's easy to remember, it is short for pessimist.

Repelling the "pests"
Pests must be avoided at all costs. You know, the religious folk who knock on the door when you're halfway through your "black pudding and chip" pizza, to ask you things like: "With all the crime and violence in the world today, what state do you think we'll be in in ten years' time?"

They are professional pests just dying to pour out the doom. They even look forward to a little abuse and tension at times. There's a way to handle them though.

It only takes one word, delivered with a smile and overwhelming enthusiasm, to have these people staggering backwards and holding up two crossed sticks as if to ward off a vampire. Let's look at our doorstep scene again.

"With all the death and destruction in our world today. What do you think the prospects are for mankind in the next decade?" The one in front is smiling thinly while her back-up nods in wise assent.

Smile broadly and reply, "Faaan-tastic!"

I guarantee you that no pest in the world can live with that word. Or Great! Or Terrific! Or any other positive expression of enthusiasm. They just don't understand it.

It could be a colleague in the office; you've just told him you're about to call on Smashitin & Bustit to sell them your latest lump hammer. He draws breath, puts on his most negative expression and starts.

"You are never going to see old man Smashitin! He has to be the meanest thing on two legs. What chance do *you* think you've got of opening an account with *him?*"

Draw yourself up to your full height and answer: *"Gr-r-reat."*

He'll wither up in front of your eyes and crawl away to try and dump his bad attitude on one of less stern character.

The truth of the matter is though, that lives can be ruined by someone else's negative opinion.

Negative comments are always more powerful than positive ones. Our minds naturally think of all the reasons why we can't achieve our goals – instead of looking for the behaviour needed to achieve them. A pest uses that power to fuel our natural fears.

The great excuses

Next time someone tells you how they can't do a thing ask them to think about how they *can* achieve it, instead. If they still can't think this way invite them to go and unload their rubbish elsewhere. With these folk you needn't be nice.

As a nation the British are looked on as great inventors. We also have the reputation for letting our inventions slip away to be developed and marketed by other countries. It is almost part of our culture to create reasons why a new design cannot be manufactured.

"The market's not ready. The time's not right. It won't sell. It'll cost too much to make. We won't get the investors."

We create alibis for doing – nothing. "It might sell in London but it definitely won't sell in the North. We can't start to move it without the brochures. The whole sales philosophy is wrong for this one. I called on them once but they didn't buy. It's too expensive". All negative thoughts, just thoughts.

Many of our better ideas remain stillborn for fear of criticism. Criticism is just another one of the numerous obstacles we will meet in life.

Obstacles are there for everyone, and it's unreal to expect that our own path won't be strewn with them, both many and varied. They only have one purpose. To sort the wheat from the chaff. There's only one way to deal with them, smash straight through. Take heart from the scientific law that Sir Isaac Newton nearly discovered: "Every obstacle has an equal and opposite solution."

Search for good solutions, not good excuses.

Opinion versus facts
Friday evening finds you down at the Bleach Drinker's Arms, quaffing the brown ale and reading the Town Centre Trumpet. You turn to the situations vacant column, look longingly at a particular job advert, and ask yourself: "Can I do it?"

Whatever your answer, either yes or no, it is not a fact, only an opinion, your own opinion but opinion nonetheless.

Never answer the "Can I?" question with a "no." You only come this way once so if you don't try everything while you're here, you'll miss it. Turn the words round and answer "I can."

So what about the salesmen who failed in business? The ones mentioned in the last chapter. Should they have stayed in their selling jobs rather than trying to be businessmen?

Of course they shouldn't! They had to try opening their own businesses. They could have succeeded, only they had pre-conditioned ideas about their roles in those businesses. They didn't manage their personal skills to the best advantage.

They had to try though. Hopefully they will have learnt

from their mistakes so that when they try again, success will be theirs.

You know what they say about people who never make mistakes? They probably lie about other things as well. To err is human and some of us are more human than others.

In the long hot summer of '76, while I was enjoying a period of dole collecting, an ageing house painter uttered these words to me.

"Fortune smiles on every man once. Take your opportunity when he does. Because the second time he sends his daughter. Miss Fortune." He was painting an ageing house at the time.

New definition of a true expert. One who has come to realise that the more he knows, the more he knows he doesn't know. Don't let someone stop you with an *expert* opinion. It's just an opinion. An adverse opinion might put you off, but no-one actually fails until he gives up trying.

Positive managing

The technique most frequently used for motivating staff, by anyone from the sales manager to the M.D., is the quaintly-termed technique of "rollicking". Telling people in no uncertain terms, what they have done wrong.

Turn it round. Start telling people what they have done right. But first of all tell them how to do it right, and tell them what right is.

There is an old term. Mushroom management. Keep your employees in the dark and keep shovelling manure on them. I am being kind when I say that much more than 50% of managers today still believe that's the way to do it. Keep 'em fearful of their jobs and they will perform well for you. Rubbish!

Life blooms much better in the full glare of the greenhouse. People are far better motivated if they can see what they are supposed to be achieving, and how that level of achievement has been arrived at, and what will happen if it is achieved.

As the sales manager, you tell your salesman that you would like him to sell £520,000 in his area this year. Tell him that that figure has been calculated by looking at the facts. Last year the same area brought in £440,000. The price increase of 10% brings that up to £484,000 and you are looking for growth of around 7.5% from his area to bring it up to the targeted mark.

You realise that it's not going to be that easy. You even admit to your salesman that the price increase and competition could lose you a customer or two. But with a potential of 25 clients in the area who are not buying your product to add to the 15 who are, you feel the targets are reachable.

You point out to the salesman what such an increase will mean to his wage packet. You also let him know that such an increase in all the company's areas will make your firm the biggest in the country. (Or third or second or whatever.) What the likely profits will be, giving him added security. And how that relates to your competitors, to whom you are determined to administer a sound smack in the gums.

You could also point out that if he did well enough, he could have your job, Sales Manager. You aren't frightened by that, because with expansion like you have in mind, you are looking to become Sales Director.

I said earlier that no-one but yourself can tell you that "you are the best." That is not true. A really good manager will make a habit of telling his top sales people how good they are. He will praise them time and time again.

Superman is just a fictional character and even number one salesman will appreciate praise, especially just after he has missed a sale and feels that it was through his own fault. It's at times like these that a "top class" manager will lift his people's self-confidence with timely reminders of their ability and past successes.

Do you let your staff see the daylight? Let them see their area sales figures? Let them see their colleagues' sales figures?

The company's figures? Your competitor's figures? They will feel far more involved if they are let in on the full picture. There should be no need for secrecy. You are all on the same side. You all succeed together.

Soft in the head

You would tell me that I'd gone soft, if I said that we should all make it a priority in life to be helpful to everyone we come in contact with.

You'd tell me that I was an idealist if I said it would make the world a better place. You would tell me that I was a dreamer if I said it would make our own lives more enjoyable to give help to others in this way. You would tell me all these things, but you would not tell me that I was wrong.

If only managers wanted to make their staff successful, there would be no need for our ministers to worry about trade figures and controls on imports from the Far East, which would otherwise flood our markets with top quality, low-priced goods. Suddenly the boot would be firmly on the other foot, with the sons of Nippon chasing around in a vain effort to match our prices and production figures.

What are you?

Hands up who wants to finish with a test? To find out how positive you are, take a glass. Half fill it with scotch. Stare at it hard. If you are unhappy that your glass is half *empty* score 0. If you are pleased that it's half *full* score 10. But if you've got fed up and emptied it down your throat then see me after class and we'll do it again, and again, and again if necessary. Until we get it right. Cheers!

4

THE MOTIVATORS

Here are four words with very similar dictionary meanings, but which are poles apart in meaning as far as salespeople are concerned. Just in case I manage to succeed in confusing you I will start by giving my own definition of the words as they relate to us salesfolk.

TARGETS – These are the projected sales figures which a salesman must achieve in order to keep his boss happy. They are imposed upon the salesman by his manager, and more often than not, the salesman has no idea how these figures are arrived at.

AIMS – These are the ambitions that the salesman is aiming for, in life. Set purely by the salesman, and for his personal satisfaction.

PLANS – The means by which the salesman organises his behaviour to achieve his personal aims in life.

GOALS – These are the sales figures and necessary behaviour to achieve those figures, worked out through discussion between the salesman and his manager. Agreed goals are one of the most powerful sales-management tools.

Targets
While aims can be as vital as breathing, targets are often as attractive as bad breath.

Your manager has just finished introducing you around

your patch, he has spent a whole week familiarising you with your products and has explained the salary plus bonus system.

You're given a target. If you achieve that target you get a bonus on everything your accounts have been invoiced for that year. But if you miss it, you get nothing. Just basic salary. Hard, but popular amongst European manufacturers.

So there you sit, watching your sales manager stride towards his LuxuryDrive V8. You are fresh and enthusiastic and you've learnt a lot. Except you're not quite sure yet how the door locks work on your company Rattlalong. You're on your own, so what's to do?

Perhaps you should take a leaf out of Brian's book. Brian is one of the most welcome salesman to electrify my door bell. He's been selling top quality German appliances for years and he's a star. I know he's a star because he tells me.

The first three months of every year finds him smashing the stuffing out of the little dimpled balls and stamping ceremoniously on freshly hewn lumps of turf, known amongst his peers as divots.

Come April and he pops in. His visits are always mutually beneficial – we do a lovely cup of coffee and in three months he's amassed a goodly selection of new jokes.

July and he's in again, he reckons that our local travel agent's got the most comprehensive list in the Midlands of flights to Ibiza. Flights to Ibiza are important to Brian because his timeshare flat is out there.

This trip he mentions the product. "Sorry to be a bore," he says, "but it wouldn't harm if you bought a half-dozen vacuum cleaners about now."

"OK Brian, put me down for twelve." They sell well and I could do with a few in stock.

"Steady Rich. Let's not rock the boat. How about six now and another six when I get back at the end of August?" smiles Brian.

So I settle on six. He goes on holiday. And I see him again

in September. Friday at two-thirty. "What's wrong Brian, I thought Friday was your golf afternoon?"

"No, we've got to sort your turnover out. I'm a bit down." He reminds me of the six other vacuums. Pours on the skills about his new washer-driers. "Take three while the offer's on." Commits me to a dozen microwaves and relaxes.

The visits are becoming regular now. Every three weeks up to December and then he skips in for a final visit the week before Christmas.

"Hello Brian, how goes it?"

"Great," says Brian. "I'm a star. I've matched my target almost exactly. In fact I'm only 1% over. My best year yet."

When Brian hits target, which he always does, he gets a pat on the back from his gaffer, his full achievement bonus, and an automatic target for next year – this year's sales value plus a bit!

He always makes sure that next year's target isn't going to be inflated by too much achievement this year.

Steve, on the other hand, was new, and tried like a trooper. His sales were 136% of target and he felt great. This year's target is 136% plus 15% but his biggest account has run off to Rio with a British Airways steward. Boy is he struggling. Worse, if he doesn't do 136+15 he gets zero bonus. Just basic rate. That's a loss in personal income of around £5800.

As the year draws on, he drops farther and farther behind target, comes round more and more often and his sunny disposition has turned as sour as the cream his bonus represented. I don't like sour cream. I start to pick up his depression. I buy a bit from him, out of sympathy. And then he's gone. Lost his driving licence when he took to drink.

So why don't targets work? Well, for a start they are set for the setter's reason, not for the salesman's. They are very rarely fair to a real trier. And worst of all they represent too long a timespan. A whole twelve months.

Setting aims

So much for targets, what about aims? "Must be self-motivated" – ever see a situations vacant advert that didn't say that? Me neither. The most effective way to motivate us is to set ourselves aims and plan to achieve them.

Setting aims works by motivating our sub-conscious to motivate our behaviour. But does it work? Yes! As sure as eggs are baby chickens.

So long as those aims can be achieved within a short time period and are exciting enough to get the adrenalin pumping.

When I was but a callow youth, my boss sent me to a seminar. It lasted a week and the two guys who ran it were pure dynamos. What they didn't know about selling hadn't come into fashion yet. And they told me all about Aim Setting.

They said that to be really effective, aims should be written down. Should be specific and should have a clear time frame. I came away knowing that this was it. The secret to successful selling. I didn't need to do anything except set a few aims and, Hey Presto! My sub-conscious would do the rest. Was I thinking BIG!

The only trouble with this theory was, I wanted so much. I spent an age specifying it all in great detail, wrote War and Peace twice over to clarify things in my mind and had the next hundred years of my life planned out with mini-targets to achieve what I wanted.

Only I forgot a few things. Getting the sack didn't help. I thought that showed total lack of understanding on my boss's part. How could I sell anything yet? The aims had to be worked out first and you can't do that in a fortnight. The seminar was his idea, for goodness sake. I had to play my part and support it.

The other thing I forgot was getting married, or rather I didn't. She vetoed the Testa Rossa, the Executive Jet, the winter month in St. Moritz, the sloop in Monte harbour, the cabin in Barbados. All for an end terrace off Scunthorpe

High Street.

I was soon thinking: "This aim setting is hopeless. It doesn't work." My next boss confirmed it. His philosophy on life was more direct.

The training I got from him consisted of one word: "Sell!"

"How?"

"Like everybody else does. Start at 7.30. Drive like a maniac all day, call on at least 50 people before you go home and tell 'em anything but... get the sale. And don't forget Saturday and Sunday, the roads are clearer and people aren't working, so they've no excuses."

He was not the nicest man I've ever met, and he hadn't finished yet. "If you want to go far in selling, young man, there's only one way. Work your backside off."

I wasn't very old but even I knew, if you did that you'd go nowhere. I mean that's what your legs are fastened to. But I worked, 12–13 hours a day, six days a week. I bought a car, a 1959 Ford Prefect and I lost a lot of hair, scratching my head. Because....

My colleague had a limousine, I knew for a fact that he never worked Wednesdays, it was his girlfriend's day off. He went away every week-end and the boss called *him* sir. It just wasn't fair, so I tackled him about it.

"Don't work more than 32 hours in any one week," he said, "40 hours only if you're pressed. Then when you're done, get playing. That way you'll feel more like working the next day."

He continued. "The trouble with most salesmen is that they don't know how to stop working. When there are lots of enquiries they go around in a frenzy like a Scotsman trying to drink every drop of whisky from a colander. And when things are slack they go even faster trying to find another bottle to pour in."

He loved a tipple and I thought I knew what he meant. Don't work hard. Work clever. Plan what *you* want to achieve.

... like a Scotsman trying to drink every drop of whisky from a colander.

So there I had it back to aims and objectives. But I felt I was on a winner so I invested in another double whisky, and listened as he poured it down his throat. Firstly I asked his opinion on the seminar I'd been to.

"Where those guys went wrong was the time scale," he said. I was all ears, which is a sight better than carrying a leg in each hand.

"Certainly aims should be specific. Aims work in our subconscious mind, to control our behaviour. And the subconscious only understands specifics. Be clear on what you want, if you can't set it down in 20 words, you haven't worked it out right."

Twenty words. I'd written thousands. "Have a Chivas Regal this time," I offered, "it's thicker, stays in the colander longer. What about writing the aims down? Do I really need to?"

"Oh yes," he continued. "I know a few chaps who have a

top pocket full of cards emblazoned with aims, they take them out at every possible opportunity and read them through, as a reminder, I used to, until I lost a wing mirror to an artic coming the other way. Where writing down is really useful though, is that it increases clarity. Makes it easy for the subconscious to absorb."

"The time scale, you said that's what the seminar guys had got wrong. Tell me about the time scale." I topped him up again and waited.

Parkinson's Law

"Aims should not have any set time scale, and I'll tell you why." He'd drunk nearly half a bottle by now but his speech was as clear as my hearing.

"Say you give yourself twelve months to earn £1500 (1963 this was). Say you do really well and by August time you've reached your target. You'd probably think that by the year end your earnings would have grown to nearly £2000. Not so. The tendency is to catch up on your paperwork, take an extra holiday, plan your next campaign, do anything but carry on selling. At Christmas you've still got your £1500 and not a penny more. It's Parkinson's law, any job you do will expand to fill completely the time you allocate to do it in.

"More likely though is that you don't take your aim seriously until it's too late to achieve it. At the start of January, December seems to be miles away. But in late October you can almost feel it breathing down your neck. Only £800 in the pot and you know you're going to miss your "aim". Now you feel bad and give up on aim-setting once and for all."

I was nodding my head so hard I shook off all the extra ears.

"But probably the biggest disadvantage to setting anything but the shortest of time scales is that things change. The market alters, your circumstances change or you simply change your aims."

Then he murmured the magic words: "Do you want to know what I do?"

Did I want to know? He had a new limousine, I had a clapped out Ford. His suit was made to measure. And the trousers matched the jacket. Mine was Sally Army bring and buy sale. Well the jacket was, I'd nicked the trousers off my dad.

What he told me went along these lines. (I've brought it up-to-date to make it more pertinent.)

First thing with aims is to keep them realistic. Say you're earning £25,000 per year, if you set yourself an aim of £50,000 it's cloud-cuckoo-land, you're used to £25,000 so twice that much is meaningless to both sides of your mind.

Set an aim that's within reach, say £30,000, and then when you get there, go for £35,000, if you want to. You might find £35,000 takes too much out of you. If it does, stop there. It's your aim, Moses didn't have it carved in tablets of stone, do what you want to do.

Secondly, keep them under your nose, things to be achieved next week or next month, not by the end of the year. Short term is the only way to bring the aims to life in your subconscious.

Thirdly, make them as real as you can. Don't think, "I want to buy a fast car next year." Think "I can just see that blonde from accounts breezing along to the flat in my new red Lotus." Don't think, "I'm going to earn £50,000 this year". Think, "I'm going to enjoy earning £4,200 this month, perhaps I should lift it to £4,500."

If you don't set "Aims", your life and career can end up being totally "aimless".

Planning

Then the conversation switched to forward planning. We agreed that people never plan to fail, they simply fail to plan.

There you sit, with your aims written down on the back of the odd envelope. Now's the time to get them all together. List down the items you want and put a value on them. Work out how much it will cost, next month, to pay the bills and buy the playthings you want. So that you know, each month or quarter or whatever, how much money you need to keep the wheels turning.

Say that your monthly costs list goes something like this:

THE BREAD AND BUTTER ITEMS	COST	TOTAL
Mortgage payments	£ 400.00	
Community charge	£ 50.00	
Insurances	£ 40.00	
Gas/Electric	£ 120.00	
Phone/T.V. Rental	£ 40.00	
Wife's Clothes	£ 80.00	
Own Clothes	£ 50.00	
Children's Allowance	£ 20.00	
Housekeeping	£ 400.00	
Pocket-Money	£ 100.00	
Motoring Tax/Insurance/ Petrol	£ 50.00	
Pension scheme	£ 200.00	
Taxes & N.I.	£1427.00	
		£2977.00
PLAYTHINGS		
Holiday	£ 300.00	
New Car	£ 289.00	
Home Improvement	£ 100.00	
Personal Computer	£ 30.00	
Meals	£ 100.00	
Weekend Breaks	£ 100.00	
Golfing Expenses	£ 70.00	
		£ 989.00
SAVINGS	£234.00	
		£ 234.00
	£4200.00	£4200.00

Make sure that the costs are accurate so that when you've achieved the aim, you can afford to reward yourself with the goodies you wanted.

Your subconscious will only work if it's fed on truth. The playthings are very important; your subconscious mind relates to real things, like a red Lotus, a fur-lined water-bed that rocks you to sleep, a high-powered stereo that will peel the paper off your neighbour's walls, much more than it does to numbers.

It's no good setting a goal of £4200 a month if you don't know why you need that amount. We can see clearly what we will do with the next £4200 we earn.

Managing activity

Now we're on the launch pad, all our aims are clear and quantified, the countdown is rolling 5 . . 4 . . 3 . . 2. " 'ere wait a mo," cries our hyped up sub-conscious, "I know where you want me to go but. . . How do I get there?"

What your sub-conscious mind needs to know now is, how to manage your activity in order to achieve your aims. And that's where the conscious mind comes in. It has to have something to do, doesn't it?

If we can show how much of our £4200 we will earn every time we make a sales contact, then we can turn that money, those aims, into actual work activity to be achieved each month. It's a simple logical exercise.

First we cast back to our past earnings and find out how much we earned for each sale achieved. Everybody is going to be different on this.

Some sales people are on pure commission, some on salary plus commission, some on salary plus bonus and some on straight salary. But we've all got averages and we all need to ensure that our sales activity can bring us the results we're looking for. In other words if you're on a straight salary which doesn't match your aims, change jobs!

You're in a showroom selling cars, each time someone

comes into the shop, or phones for a price, or writes in for a brochure, that's a contact.

If you're out on the road selling Electric Drills, Greeting Cards, Pacemakers, Micro-computers, whatever, every time you walk into someone's office and show them your face, that's a contact.

Most salespeople are on a commission-related salary, which is the best system for aim-motivation. So we look back and find that over the last ten months we earned a monthly average of £4200 from ten sales. What a convenient average, £420 in our pocket for every sale achieved.

Now we need to know how many qualified presentations we made to achieve our ten sales, our conversion rate. This is probably the most flexible ratio in a salesman's vocabulary.

JIM	"So what's your conversion rate then?"
FRED	"Oh around 50%. What's yours?"
JIM	"Well that sounds a bit on the low side, mine's more like 75%. What's yours Bill?"
BILL	"Last month we converted 100% but usually it's more like 80%."
JIM	"Cripes! That's good. What's yours Tom?"
TOM	"Mine's a Campari, with soda. And plenty of ice."

Well mine's 33%. So we divide our £420 per sale by 3 to find out how much we earn every time we present our goods to a qualified prospect. £140, whether they buy or not! If we can present to 30 prospects each month, we'll earn £4200.

Your aim however is £4500 for the next month. Which relates to 3 more presentations. You have to ask yourself, "Can I do 33 presentations this month." If you want to, you will.

Take this logic one step further, and ask yourself how many sales contacts you have to make to secure a qualified presentation. Say that figure is 4.

For every four couples who walk into the showroom, you get one opportunity to present your wares. Offer them all a coffee, they're worth £35 to you. (£140 per presentation divided by 4 calls per presentation.)

So here we are, in our hypothetical situation, every time we find somebody who's warm and breathing we will earn £35. Everytime we tell him our story we will earn £140. Everytime we get his autograph on a cheque it's worth £420.

If the numbers are all wrong for you, so what! They're my numbers. I won't sulk if you put your own in there.

The whole object of this exercise is to manage your activity properly, to give your sub-conscious a route to follow and to satisfy your needs for cash and playthings. Nobody's going to mind if you get it a bit wrong, they're your aims to do with as you please. Now there's freedom for you.

Goals

Let's go back to that sales manager stepping quietly into his LuxuryDrive V8. Seven years of selling under his belt and he's just let a man out on the road with seven days training and a list of accounts that his predecessor looked after. And the hope that his man comes up with decent sales figures.

His target, for the areas he looks after, has been bothering him for the last month. The market is tight and his sales director is panicking. The board is beginning to sniff for blood. What is in doubt is whose blood that will be. So he's off to the pub to worry.

Then the sales manager decides to sit down with his new salesman, and have a talk.

They study the new man's territory. He has 25 accounts to visit. Plus 11 accounts who have left the fold. Plus 130 potential accounts who don't know what the fold looks like.

They discuss a programme of motivational visits to the existing accounts, calls to try and repair the damage to those who no longer deal. And pure sales visits to the potentials.

They agree where the new salesman is going every day next

week. What type of presentation he is going to give on each visit. They agree on the time to talk each evening so that the experienced man can hear the new boy's report, praise and advise him. And they set a time on Friday to meet and plan for the week to come.

They set agreed goals for action and the manager monitors that action.

Then the sales manager visits the sales director. The director has been in the business for fifteen years and he's good. They talk. They study the present state of trade. They discuss the behaviour necessary to motivate the desired results from each area.

They agree on what that behaviour should be and set their goals to achieve the desired results. Then they agree the times for the manager to report to his director by phone and set up the next eyeball to eyeball meeting. At the end of the month.

Now watch our new salesman stroke his car into life each Monday morning. He knows where he's going as soon as the heater has demisted the windscreen, because he agreed it with his boss.

He knows what he needs to achieve on these visits. Because he's agreed that with his boss. And he knows what behaviour to employ to best achieve the desired results. Because he's agreed that with his boss too.

He knows he has to speak to his boss this evening, and is looking forward to relating his successes. The failures will be thrashed out on Friday afternoon in the weekly face to face. He also knows that he has to stick to his agreements, because his boss gets very touchy if he doesn't.

But more than that, he feels more confident now that his own seven days of experience have been expanded by seven years of his manager's experience plus fifteen years input from his director.

What chance do those potential customers stand trying to resist an onslaught like that?

Motivation takes many forms, but targets, like wage rises

are not strong motivators.

Aims will keep you going on those wet Wednesday afternoons when you've just drawn your sixth: "Not today thank-you," in a row and you are sat in the car waiting for the AA to come and mend your second puncture of the week, thinking: "Why do I do this?"

Flick open your case, look at the picture of your family. This usually spurs you on, but not today. Take out the list of playthings you have promised yourself. Read down to the "second honeymoon in Cannes" that will happen in June. Then scan the next aim: a pair of laser powered sun-glasses that guarantee you can look at all those bronzed twenty-year-olds while a picture of your eyes, projected onto the lenses, is looking in the opposite direction.

Planning what to do is the only way to get it done in time.

And finally, setting goals is the most efficient way for the manager to manage his staff's behaviour. There is a very beneficial side effect, too. Where goals are agreed, both become far more involved in the company.

5

CLOTHE THAT SALE

For a long time it was believed that the spoken word was the most important form of communication. We may use facial expression, gestures and touch, but sales trainers taught us that words alone express our needs and thoughts and that unless we can master the art of speech and language we will find it difficult to communicate effectively.

Business schools put communication in first place in their curricula. They taught us that unless we could communicate effectively, we could not expect to run a successful business nor indeed be able to take our proper place in everyday life.

But words alone will not do. First we must make sure our customers are listening properly. Our customer's reaction to our words is more directly related to what goes on inside their mind than what comes out of our mouth. In any meeting with a fellow human being – when we are trying to describe ideas, feelings, thoughts and information – our ability to communicate effectively will be based:-

10% on what we say.
30% on how we sound when we are saying it.
60% on how we look when we are saying it.

Imagine we are involved in a sales presentation, a job interview, training sessions, dealings with our staff and colleagues, or even just social and family occasions. It won't count one jot what we say if we look wrong because the chance of our prospect accurately hearing what we say is minimal.

60% is the way we look

You are a home architect. Carl and Janine Doublebarrel-Buyer have had some trouble parking. There was room on the lot for as many Fiat Unos as you like but it proved impossible to get the Roller tethered without a slight redesign to the front bumper, which became passionately attached to an innocent Honda moped. Anyhow they have made it.

They heard all about you in the flowery editorial you bought in the county magazine. Their ambition is to become your new record spender. They browse the displays and are impressed with your artistry in creating pseudo-country-cottage interiors more authentic than they have seen in any of their friends' houses.

They are approached by David the designer. David wears turquoise spectacles, a stonewashed denim shirt, black checked tie, small drop of glue on his right temple where his pony tail toupee is secured. Large CND ear-ring in his left nostril, muddy motor bike boots and the half-grown beard he is cultivating to try and smother the acne that's taken squatting rights on his feeble jawbone.

It was his 50cc Honda that has now become the rather garish, outer deflector shield to their nutmeg Corniche, but he can't claim that as an excuse.

Designer David speaks, "Hello. How may I help you?"

Carl can't quite believe his eyes and does not reply. He hasn't even heard the question. He is thinking "My God! This creature has an ear-ring in its nose."

"Have you come to look at lounge interiors, swimming pools, or is it a whole house scheme you're interested in?" David's second try.

"I'm not having those muddy boots across my off-white

"My God! This creature has an ear-ring in its nose."

Wilton," ponders Janine. But not wishing to appear rude she replies, "Well ... err ... Carl, the young man's speaking to you."

"Fire-places."

"Fine. And would you like a character inglenook with oak beams, or an Adam-style pine unit?" Dave is struggling on manfully.

"I bet he's one of those Goonies. Just look at that shirt." Again Carl's concentration is not on the question to hand. "Sorry, what was that?"

"Do you want oak or pine?"

"Yes." Pause. "Do you have any brochures?" Janine begins the escape ploy.

"Certainly. I'll go and fetch you some." David dives dutifully into the office to gather them some leaflets. Carl and Janine are in the Roller before he's had a chance to return.

Designer David is the best in the business. Bar none. He had exactly what Carl and Janine desired. If only they had started to communicate. He didn't look right so the Doublebarrel-Buyers roll into the car park at Seller Sids.

Seller Sid, or Salty as his friends call him, wears a dark blue suit, white shirt, blue tie with tiny silver and red squares, has a red rosebud pinned to his lapel and a flamboyant matching handkerchief carefully arranged in his breast pocket. His shoes are aglow with black polish and the only thing he wears on his face are his eyebrows. All this is topped off with a sparse helping of grey locks which just ooze experience.

What he actually knows about interior design wouldn't come past the mud on David's boots but he gets the chance to tell Carl and Janine his story. He looks right. He has every chance of getting the business.

Then there was that day you were in the office. Since breakfast you have been trying to off-load three third-hand B.M.W.s and a dented Porsche to the local motor dealers, and clear your forecourt for the Mercedes and Jaguars you sell. It's making you sweat a little.

It's the secretary's day off. Your colleague is joy-riding with a client, the mechanics have been out on a "tow-in" all morning and the cleaner went home during your attempts to wash the orange juice stain out of your best Jaguar saloon's seat – the one that darling little four-year-old made last week.

You would have had this challenging project finished if it wasn't for the constant interruptions. And then, in he comes, straight into the showroom.

Bib overalls that were white once. Woolly cap which had its origins as a tea cosy and is rapidly becoming thatched in a psychedelic mixture of mummified emulsion and artex. Matching string bootlaces. White spotted spectacles. Collar-length grease that is strangling his hair and thick black smoke gushing from the queerest pipe you've ever seen. Your first impression is that he is a scrap dealer, who has lost his way.

You try and duck back behind the office door but it's no good. He's seen you. He speaks with an accent that's so thick you reach for your French phrase book.

You realise that his mother tongue is a quaint form of English deformed by the groove that his pipe has burned into his off-brown teeth, at just about the same time you notice the truck he has abandoned on the double yellows outside your front window.

It's a sort of green and rust two tone with red lead flashes and an engineering modification which relies on string knotted around the window winder and snaking suggestively over the cab to secure the silencer shaped rust clot that sits at the back of the exhaust pipe.

You slouch out of the office trying to focus your mind on something to admire in the man, and start your opening sales gambit.

Then the phone rings. You stop and hesitate. He's warm and walking so you've got to think of him as a customer. At that moment your colleague arrives back. The relief. You go for the phone and jerk your thumb to the showroom. "Someone has just come in, Col."

Your colleague finds out that the painted prospect is a slightly eccentric master decorator, who has just been left a rambling farm estate, and a whole lot of loose change, in his millionaire uncle's will.

Col Heague sells him two of the new Jaguar saloons, in matching colours, one for him and one for the missus and a pair of Mercedes sports cars for his son and son-in-law.

Col's commission pays for 4 weeks on Bali and a fuel injected Nisda 2.8i Ghia.

Your own morning's toil netted £1,800. For one of the BMs and a boil the size of a hen's egg on your dialling finger. So now you know that you can't make judgments on looks alone. But it has just cost you a packet to prove that all of us do.

Think of the last time you interviewed someone for a job. How long had they been in the room before you had weighed them up. Two minutes? Half an hour?

I bet you were thinking, "She looks O.K." or, "I don't like the look of this one." Before they had cleared the office doorway. Judgments are instantaneous.

People will hear what we say only if they listen to us, and if
we don't look good there is a 60% chance they won't take in
what we say. So how do we look good?

How to look right
Speaking for the ladies, I haven't a clue. Sorry girls but I
know my limitations. In any case saleswomen are far better
dressers than men. So I asked a saleslady what she looked for
in a well-presented man.

(Before anyone starts nailing themselves to railings I
should point out that I'm neither Feminist, Maleist, Sexist or
Sexy if it comes to that. However I do know when I'm under-
qualified.)

"It is so easy for a salesman to be well turned out. First rule
is good grooming. Hair washed daily, white teeth, clean
fingernails. Then I look for style. Someone who is under
rather than overdressed and, most important, someone
whose clothes are co-ordinated.

"If you will be dealing with business people in the upper-
middle class bracket aim for that look. Wear a suit and
waistcoat, always with a silk tie and handkerchief and the
crispest white shirt you can find.

"When it comes to business suits, it's worth splashing out
on top quality, wool or wool blend, in blue, medium or dark
grey. Apart from lasting longer, quality fabric will keep its
shape better and stop you developing a tired and bedraggled
look.

"If you're not thrilled at the prospect of buying lots of
expensive suits, you can easily build a co-ordinated wardrobe
inexpensively. Choose three basic colours for the trousers.
Blue, grey and black; look at the labels to make sure they are
washable and then only wear them two or three times before
washing and pressing. Always keep the creases sharp,
nothing looks worse than a shapeless leg.

"Then build up a collection of shirts, jackets and pullovers
to co-ordinate with the three colours. Men bother far less

han women about co-ordinating their clothes and really that
s the secret."

"O.K." I interrupted, "but selling is a bit creative. Most
alesmen would like to look a little flamboyant. How would it
be if we dressed with flair?"

"Fine but keep it toned down."

Then she suggested, "To get a flamboyant look, how about
black trousers in the latest style and with a perfect crease,
crisp white shirt, black shoes and, to top it off a bow tie. Very
smart, a bit different and you can't offend anyone. Then if
you have your hair in one of the more gentle modern styles,
your 'flair' look should be complete.

"If it's mid-summer and sweltering, you can go for light
green trousers, again the crease, white "grandad" shirt with
matching green pinstripe, open at the neck, and shoes that
match the trousers. Or accessorise it all around cream or light
blue trousers instead. If you want jewellery, keep it at an un-
noticeable level. You don't want to look like a second-hand
car salesman, unless you sell second-hand cars.

"The great shame is that so many salesmen do not take the
trouble with their appearance that they should. They feel that
a visit to a *real* hair stylist will brand them limp wristed or
they simply can't be bothered with all the fuss. It is so
important. After all we're not door-to-door fishmongers, yet
so many men dress as if they were."

I glanced in the mirrored ceiling, and winced.

Looking good makes you feel good
Apart from the effect this well-dressed and well-groomed
appearance will have on other folk, it will also make the most
macho man feel better about himself. And we all know that
feeling good brings us better results.

Less macho types usually share the ladies' sensitivity in
dress sense anyhow. If you dress in the manner of the person
you wish to become, you are a good way towards getting
there.

So good clothes, well pressed and colour co-ordinated. Well groomed hair. And so to the face.

There is a fashion amongst those of us who wear specs to go for something unusual. Heavy glasses or coloured frames. Wrong. People won't hear you if their brain is occupied with the face furniture. Try contact lenses. Or no-rim lightweights.

Perhaps the finest are the gold rimmed half specs that you can peep over; very authoritative when accompanying grey hair. Dress like someone people will take notice of.

What about a beard, or moustache? Hair is hair and too much of it is a barrier. Only wear face hair if you keep it super neat.

Now take bad breath and body odour. Well I don't want 'em. And neither does anyone else. Unless you want to demonstrate mouth fresheners or deodorants there is nothing professional about smelling bad. In fact, if you are guilty of these traits, you have to label yourself as a *rank* amateur.

Remember, 60% of your impact on customers is visual and there's only one chance to make a good first impression. That's why I avoid appointments before lunchtime. It takes that long to fix the cracks in the mirror!

Body language

The much vaunted subject of Body Language is a different thing. Whether it actually means anything significant that the person who is promising you a commitment is rubbing the inside of his collar with his forefinger, or sitting with his chin cupped in one hand, his victory fingers pointing up his cheek, is open to great debate.

It has become accepted that a single gesture cannot be interpreted, but that a sequence of actions may well be indicative of an unspoken thought.

If she has not once looked you in the eye, is constantly checking the wrist where she has forgotten to put her watch and listens to you with her back turned, eyeballing the traffic passing by outside, the chances are that she has lost all interest in what you are saying.

Keeping your eye on the unspoken indicators can be very useful if you are speaking to a group of clients. You may be aiming your presentation at the Managing Director but notice that each time you go for a trial close, and ask him for a commitment, he glances to his financial director for back-up.

You are aiming at the wrong man. Your presentation should be re-tuned to suit the financial director who, it seems, is going to make the final decision on this one.

This also applies when a salesman is presenting to a man and wife. So often the salesman will aim his presentation at the husband and when wife asks a question he will answer it by talking to the husband. Even worse, he may ignore the question until it is re-asked by the man. Wife at this point feels so offended that she wouldn't even buy his free offer. This happens a lot.

Sexual discrimination takes many forms, make sure you don't fall foul of this one. If you listen to wife, she'll love you for it, ignore her and she'll hate you and give her money to a more sensitive salesman.

Keep your eyes on the customers' reactions to help you understand what they are saying; whether that is a studied knowledge of body language, or the fact that you have enough grey matter to realise what is happening, is open to some debate.

6

ACCENT ON SALES

The disco lights are flashing, on the edge of the dance floor Sheila Shaknshimmy has spotted me. And tonight I'm hot.

Sheila shuffles clear of her pals to get a better view. She sees me looking. Her eyes smoulder, her knees turn liquid at the thought that, perhaps, I might approach. She has never seen a more handsome figure of a man. (If you don't stop laughing I'll finish right here!)

Sure enough dreamboat saunters forward. Sheila smiles, and steps carefully to one side of her friends, girating like a sextet of sioux, around the heap of Marks and Spencer's designer handbags. The very air in the disco sparks in the sexual tension.

Our eyes embrace in the opening turmoil of a night to be filled with molten passion and unbridled lust.

And then the dream opens his mouth.

Having had a jar or two of Theakstons, dream sounds like a demented Crippen with psychopathic tendencies and brain damage, "Waana danse ven darlin?" Sheila's watery knees gush upwards and wash her smouldering eyes with tears of laughter as she changes her mind and rejoins the bags.

The right sound
Enough of this levity. Our customers will form an opinion on what we say, mainly from the way we look. But the second

greatest impact will be how we sound.

Academic studies have proven conclusively that 30% of
our effectiveness as communicators will rely on our sounding
good. Which means that for a salesperson, it is more
important to learn how to sound right, than it is to learn what
to say.

Yet even the words "to sound right" have an infinitely
flexible meaning. A pickled Lemming salesman on an East
End market has no need of a Hoxford haccent. But to move
the same product in the Harrods food hall requires R's
rounder than glamour girl's photogenic features.

The television advertisers, who hold sway over so much
mass opinion these days would have us believe that; to sell
butter you must be able to "Ooh-Argh" like a west country
yokel. Fibre-rich bread needs a command of the Lancashire
phrase "Ee were a gwate baker were 'r daad." While to sell
the news on either channel needs best BBC British. ·

Then there is the airline pilot. He has to be cool, laid back
and totally confident that the tonnes of metal we are all
entombed in will not hit the ground until he tells it to. He
needs an endless drawl and lots of "errrr's". Here is the
British Airways captain who flew us to Dusseldorf last year.

(To be read at half the normal speed.)

"Errrr ... good .. morning .. ladies and gentlemen .. errr.
This is Captain Bumpdown speaking errrr .... we are
cruising .. at errr .. 33,000 feet .. errr and at the moment ...
we are passing over Amsterdam .. errrr ... We will be errr ...
beginning our descent in errrr .. 10 minutes errr .. and should
be landing at .. errrr .. errrr .. errr."

At this point he switched off the address system to check
his road map – "Dusseldorf errr .. at about half past twelve ..
local time ... errr. Enjoy your errrr ... trip."

All these different professions have realised that an
identifiable sound is a great asset, it will have the same effect
in our profession. So, as a good voice is so important we
ought to take a stab at defining what goes to make up the
right sound.

... he switched off the address system to check his road map.

Accent

In Britain, the most accepted accents are the less extreme ones. Home Counties, the Scottish burr and the soft and gentle Irish lilt.

My own favourite is the soft clip from the natives of Tyneside though I'm told that Geordie is as unfashionable as Scouse; Brummie; extWeem Public School; Sloane, "o.k. ya," and t' thees, thous an t'uthers of the Tyke.

All perfectly acceptable if used in the immediate location but, if you have an extreme accent, and want to deal with the Doublebarrel-Buyers of this world it can do no harm to hone your accent into a gentler mode.

How? Practise your speech into a tape recorder, try and identify the harsher noises that you make and practise, practise, practise to polish them out.

It is no good taking the negative view and convincing yourself that you can do nothing about your accent. Professional actors do.

Many actors and actresses will tell you that their daily speech patterns have been developed by a few years at acting school.

They may even have enrolled on a course of elocution lessons, to polish their speech into a beautifully rounded voice. If they then land a part in a film or T.V. soap opera they may be asked to speak in a country dialect or an alien accent. Actors can do this without a slip. Actors are only people like you and me. In fact some of the best salesmen I know are actors.

Any edge you can steal on your competition is worth cultivating.

Another little flaw that a tape recorder will highlight is the words you over-use, especially if you have the recording typed out afterwards. You normally end up with a very confused typist and more repeats than the BBC in August. Do it, if nothing else you will give yourself a good laugh.

Speed

More important to how we sound is the speed at which we speak.

It is a safe bet that the vast majority of us, in all the excitement of a sales presentation, speed up our speech pattern from its normal rate of around 190 words per minute.

If our rush of adrenalin has brought that nearer the 400 word mark then we will lay ourselves open to the accusation of *fast talking* our customers into the sale. Tut, tuts all round. Except from those of you furiously counting the rate at which you speak.

Probably the greatest drawback though, to being a fast talker, is that we regularly find ourselves saying things we haven't thought about yet.

The fact is, of course, that we all talk at different rates; to be really in empathy with our customers we could try and talk at the same rate as they do.

A fast talker will soon become bored and impatient if we

speak in slow and measured tones. But a slow speaker will feel pushed, mistrustful and agitated if we reel off our prose with all the rush of pearls from a broken necklace.

Chances are that if we can speak at the same rate as they do we will sound right to them. If that's too much to expect, then slower is better. We know how little the words we use contribute to the sale, so practising, "do you want to buy?" at different speeds of speech should be within reach of everyone.

What really wreaks havoc, to conversation and communication, is speedy speech linked together with a super-broad accent.

Variety is the spice of speech

The safest bet is to vary the speed at which we speak. It gets monotonous all round if you spend half the presentation trying to jerk your prospect back out of a deep slumber. Varying the rate of speech will guarantee optimum attention from your listener.

It's surprising how we can emphasise our most pertinent points with a practised pause. Guaranteed to snap our prospect's mind into focus, with a panicky thought "Ooh, he's stopped talking, it must be my turn, I wonder what he was on about, what shall I say?" These pauses also give us the chance to start listening to him but I'll come to the importance of that later.

Inflection

Any good conversationalist will be superb at the art of stressing words and syllables to emphasise the meaning of his words. Anyone who is poor at this, and speaks in the same old monotone will be a boon for insomniacs.

Just for a bit of fun read out aloud the following sentence, stressing the word highlighted. See how the whole meaning changes when the inflection is moved from word to word, along the line.

I don't believe he said that about you. (Someone else

believes that he uttered those dreadful words, not me.)

I *don't* believe he said that about you. (It's no good, you won't convince me that he said such a thing.)

I don't *believe* he said that about you. (Brother do I know he said it?)

I don't believe *he* said that about you. (I know exactly who it was that said it and it wasn't him.)

I don't believe he *said* that about you. (I know very well that he is thinking it but he doesn't have the nerve to say it.)

I don't believe he said *that* about you. (All right so he said something, but not that.)

I don't believe he said that about *you*. (You are just being paranoid, he was actually talking about me!)

Inflection is one of the most powerful ways of changing the meaning of the words we use. As such it deserves special awareness.

Volume

Any good quality stereo amplifier will have a volume control; it is something that a great many salespeople could do with.

All too regularly a salesman presenting his wares to a customer will raise his voice to try and emphasise his points. Let that poor customer try to butt in and clarify a point and he raises it another notch or two. He usually speeds up as well, in order to get his point home before his client can stop him. It's a good point you see. He has just thought it up and no-one is going to stop him presenting it.

By this time the client is feeling under stress and maybe just a shade afraid. Only people who don't like you will shout at you. Next time you want to get a really telling point over, whisper.

If you are in a room full of people and someone is whispering, everyone listens. They feel that the only reason you could have for whispering is that you have a secret to tell, and boy do they want to share it.

Your clients will have to concentrate on what you are

saying if you are saying it quietly. Don't force your words on them, rather make them strain a little to hear you.

Silence
The only sound more powerful than a whisper is silence itself. Your presentation is going well, but yours is a complicated product.

You understand it perfectly, but perhaps you are rushing it a bit and you lost your client just after you had confirmed their name.

You have been doing all the talking and it is pretty clear that they are drifting off into their own thoughts. Probably wondering what they are going to have for lunch.

The only way to get them back is to pause. Shut up. The silence will evade their muse and cause them to feel uncomfortable. Silence has to be filled, it cannot go on for long.

You will get a question and the chance to start again.

Remember 30% of your effectiveness as a communicator depends on the way you sound to your clients. Only 10% is down to the words you use. Learn how to say it before you learn what to say.

And if you're still not convinced it is that important to sound right, ask yourself why Mrs. Thatcher, with all the power and influence that she commands, has had elocution lessons aimed at toning down her strident voice.

7

THE WORD'S WORTH

I have spent a lot of time on communicating. It is the life-blood of a good salesperson. I have covered the facts that 50% of our effectiveness as a communicator relies on the way we look, that 30% is the way we sound, and now we're going to look at that final 10%: the words we use.

If such a small percentage of our effect as communicators is due to the actual words that we use – why should we bother with learning what to say? It cannot be very important.

Of course that's not so. Saying the right thing is vital. We are in such a competitive market that being at a 10% disadvantage is enough to see us starving. If the successes are only the tip of an elephant's trunk better than the failures, then 10% represents the whole beast.

Let's go back to the very first thing I said in this book. "People buy on emotion and justify afterwards with facts."

Dream words
Our customers do not buy the product from us, they buy the dreams set out on the pages of a glossy brochure. They buy the good feeling brought about by the reaction of their friends and relatives, to their purchase. They buy the joy created by what our product can do for them.

We sell the *benefit to them* of our products and services.

This logic has brought about the development of the

phrase which every sales trainer in the land teaches:-

"Don't sell the feature, sell the benefit."

And all the sales trainers are in agreement on how to do this. We should all learn to use the words: "Which means that."

Sell the feature *which means that* benefit.

Sheila Softnbouncy walks into the furniture department of her favourite high street store, she's had her old bed for almost eight years and her springs have gone. She walks up to the sales assistant and explains her need for a really good bed. "It'll be our second anniversary soon and the bed's worn out, show me what you've got."

Arthur the assistant shows her and finishes his sales pitch with: "This particular bed has 2000 individual pocket springs (feature) which means that it will never go saggy (benefit), you won't find yourself rolling towards the middle (benefit – except for newlyweds) and it will support every square inch of your body to give you the most comfortable night's sleep imaginable (main benefit)."

That's OK for our competitors, but in today's market the "features which means benefits" concept is second-best.

We are selling the dream; we need to generate an emotional reaction. The only way to achieve this is with descriptive phrases.

We need to paint clear pictures in our clients' minds. Pictures that match their every emotion. Pictures that they cannot resist. We should use words which appeal to their senses.

Bed salesman: "Let me show you this beautiful four-poster, see the craftsmanship that's gone into that stitching, feel how comfortable it is, you'll sleep like a princess on this bed. And imagine how secure and cosy you'll feel when you draw the curtains around you to keep the rest of the world at bay on those frosty winter nights, just you and your husband, together, in complete peace."

Furniture salesman: "*Look* at the beauty of this oak

dresser. *Touch* it, *feel* the quality of the finish. Open the cupboard. *Smell* the wood."

Cooker salesman: "Just look how many different foods you can cook together in this new oven. Can't you just *taste* those steaks, sizzling under the grill?"

Touch, smell, sight, sound and taste are all effective in the sale of our products. Do you use them?

I know one kitchen dealer whose wife baked bread every Saturday morning, in one of the display ovens. His customers remarked on how great his showroom smelled because of it. They associated his kitchens with the smell of fresh baked bread.

Make sure your customers handle the goods so that they can feel the quality. If you are selling jewellery or clothes or shoes, get the customer to try them on. Not to see if they fit, but to tempt them into keeping them on when they see how good they look.

Making your clients feel good is making the sale.

Your clients will feel good about you, if you offer them a coffee or a little wine, to help them to relax. Make sure you're well insured though. I know of one client who became so relaxed she fell off her chair.

The "describe the dream" rule doesn't just apply between the retailer and his customer, it is equally true between the manufacturer and the retailer.

Tractor salesman to a prospective dealer: "As one of our dealers, you'll sleep a lot better knowing that we undertake to deliver any damages or shortages within seven days; all your customers will be happy with that.

"Plus we have our own team of technicians who will organise to install the replacement parts for you. No matter who is at fault. Think of the time that will save you on service jobs. Think of the extra profit from your increased selling time. Think of the Caribbean beaches and those extra sundrenched holidays you will have time to take."

Doesn't that sound better than: "We have our own team of

service fitters (feature) which means that once you have sold
the machine you can forget about any service jobs (benefit)".
Come to think of it either way, it sounds like a dealer's dream!

The "features which mean benefits" method should be
shelved – until after the sale and then used to help your
customers to justify their purchase. Which is still a very
important role.

Find out the real reason why your customers want to buy,
think about the emotional reaction you should generate to
match that reason, and then use the descriptive words needed
to generate that reaction.

Keep it simple

There must be thousands, nay hundreds of thousands, of
words in the English language. All through our school life,
from infants to sixth form, we are taught to use them. In fact
those with a comprehensive command of the English
language are rated amongst the cleverest people in the land.
Fine. Let's all stand up and clap those people.

But while we do let's remember. It will do no good at all if
we have a comprehensive knowledge of every word there ever
was, or is likely to be, if the person we are speaking to is a
linguistic ignoramus. It doesn't matter one jot what we say,
what matters is what our customer *thinks* we have said.
Which brings me on to jargon.

Jargon

Every trade has it, everyone uses it. We want to paint dream
pictures in the minds of our customers, dreams they cannot
resist. Jargon paints blank pictures. Use words which your
customer can relate to.

"This car has twin overhead cams, a three stage turbo
charger, transistorised ignition and the latest bosch engine
management system," smiles Superior Stephen, stepping
back smugly.

"Our Gert's new car has got a little black box that saves her etrol, will mine have?" Asks Doris Doughaplenty.

"Cretin," thinks Stephen.

"You're not getting my money," thinks Doris, "I can't nderstand a word you say, you're trying to trick me!"

As for technical details, forget them. Unless you're selling o scientists or school teachers who live and breathe facts, igures and chemical formulae. They will demand to know he additives and preservatives which make up the base con- tituents of our products. Plus their long-term effects on the nternal organs of a white rat.

In this case forget the customer. That type can seriously lamage your health.

Technical details don't paint pictures, they will leave your lient's mind empty. Always describe your wares in "feeling" words. Great is better than Polygodnozwot Resin. Fabulous s better than injection moulded.

Salesman says: "This washing machine holds 4.5kg of washing." His buyer nods off.

She'll stay awake though if he suggests that: "This machine vill take your whole coloured wash for a full week, giving you he certainty that you will always have the children's avourite clothes ready in the morning. That'll make sure hey have nothing to moan about and that you have a peaceful breakfast."

Only ever use technical details to support an emotional eaction. They are the features which must be turned into a benefit, even then turn the technical data into something your lient can relate to. Nobody cares if an oven is 80,000 cubic centimetres, but they will be interested to know that: "This very spacious oven will hold a 32 lb turkey which means plenty of room for the family dinner on Christmas day."

Whether you are dealing with doctors, accountants, bank managers, whoever, straightforward language will always be he most effective.

Control the conversation

I've mentioned before that one of my passions in life is motor car racing. One of the best respected writers on that subject has often pointed out that the very fastest drivers were the ones who used the minimum power necessary for them to go around a corner quickly. In other words their wheels weren't spinning or sliding and losing grip because they were applying excess power during cornering.

The same logic applies in selling. The best salespeople are the ones who use the least number of words to achieve their sales. They are careful that those words consist of prompts and questions, including of course the most pertinent question of all: "Do you want to buy?"

Without the self-confidence of a top salesperson, it is quite difficult to follow this route. Customer stops talking, salesperson panics and prattles on ad infinitum.

You will find that if you allow your customer to do enough talking, he will often talk himself into the sale, sometimes with absolutely no help from you. He will certainly answer an awful lot of his own objections, if you give him the chance.

"I don't like a wooden head-board on my bed," moans Michael Hardtoplease: "Mind you, that mahogany does look superb. Perhaps I'll get used to it. Yes I think I'd like a mahogany bedhead. Put it on my order." If you stay quiet and let him get on with it you can be fresh to tackle the real objections when they crop up.

You will control the presentation with prompts, questions and careful use of silence. If you want to practise any sales patter, practise phrases like: Tell me about... How do you feel about... What are your thoughts on.... Plus the classics: Do go on... Oh, tell me more.. and Uh, uh...

Reaction words

Eye-to-eye contact should always accompany verbal communication. It is the best indicator that what you are saying is hitting home. If their eyes are dull and listless and always

... you know you're not getting through.

darting over to the pub sign across the street, you know you're not getting through.

Similarly if their eyes snap sharply into focus when you mention a particular word or phrase or name, then you know that you have either lit them up or you have hit a nerve.

You: "Even estate agents are now agreeing that a luxury bathroom adds value to a home. Not that I have much respect for what estate agents say!" If his eyes snap sharply from the torpor that has beset them, then the chances are that he sells houses for a living and you've just lost a sale.

We all differ, in our views, experiences and personality. Some folk you can joke with, others are as serious as sour cream. Some would enjoy your flirting with them; others would be deeply offended. You can soon find yourself on thin ice. But then behaviour that is a little out of the norm can help you sell a lot of goods.

If your style is flamboyant, and it should be, you must watch the reaction that your style and your words have on people. If you do hit a reaction word, if their eyes start to dart about nervously, searching for the exit, don't use it again. Steer well clear; it won't help your cause.

Unless they are nodding off! If you perceive that your prose is flowing past their eardrums with no lasting effect, throw in a reaction word. Like "condom". It will guarantee that you become the focus of their undivided attention.

If you do decide to throw in a reaction word, keep it within the privacy of your own premises and make sure your listener is a consenting adult.

Foul language and blasphemous words will almost certainly bring on a bad reaction.

Communicating clearly is one of the hardest things for a human being to do well. It helps if you know what effect the way you look, how you sound and what you say, has on your customers.

It is certain that a good salesperson has to be as expert in face-to-face communication as President Reagan was at mass communication. That skill, and probably that skill alone, kept him in the most powerful job on the planet!

8

RESPECT

In Britain, the word 'salesman' conjures a picture in most consumers' minds of a fast talking, shifty-eyed individual with a thin waxed moustache, wearing dark glasses, black and white brogues and a loud striped suit.

The archetypal spiv. Spiv's major skill was his gift of the gab; his pitch; his patter; his spiel; his chat. Call it what you will, it was all mouth work. He could make his mouth say anything, he would lie, cheat and con his customers into buying his wares.

The archetypal spiv.

He is the reason why the most important job in the land is looked upon, by our customers, with such scant respect.

The punter
Well, if they don't respect you, why should you respect them? Why should you see the folk who flock through your showroom doors or invite you into their offices, as anything more than "Punters?"

They will lie and stall and waste your valuable time – promise you future orders when they have no intention of buying – try to weedle free samples or a free meal out of you and then go back to your competitor for the goods; little wonder that so many salespeople, me included, often look upon the customer as the enemy.

It is this attitude that makes our business a kind of war, they meet you as the enemy, thinking that you are out to con them; you in turn feel suspicious of their motives and believe they are simply out to waste your time. Not a good atmosphere to build trust and rapport.

You can sell in these conditions but it ain't easy and it's certainly no fun, not for you and not for them.

Life's too short to be miserable all the time, so if you intend to earn your living by selling, then you are forced to find ways of turning the war into a fun experience. The best way to do that is to find ways to respect the "punter."

Honesty
Perhaps the greatest respect you can show to anyone is to be honest with them.

Honesty is always the best policy – it is! I'm sure it is you know. Well I think it is. Come on, let's be honest, it isn't. If you go through life being totally honest in everything you say and do, you will sell so much that you will become the country's leading expert at filling in dole forms.

Mrs. Customer: "Do you think these turquoise shoes go with my bright red dress and my puce green hat, do they look all right?"

Honest Joe: "Oh great missus, for someone who is completely colour-blind and devoid of all taste."

I'm not advocating becoming an outright liar, but honesty has to be a matter of degree and when the opportunity arises to tell the kind lie, we'd all be stupid to pass it up. Whether that kindness is aimed at taking the pressure off the customer or taking pressure off us.

I'm told that a good liar needs a first-class memory, which puts me out of the game. I can't even remember what I say when I tell the truth. So I have a solid reason to avoid contrived lies. I had a colleague once, who was hooked on lying.

He asked me to go to a local doctor's surgery one morning, to fill in the details on an order he had just secured. It was Thursday. The day before had been my day off, only colleague had found it easier to tell the doctor that I had been off ill. Don't ask me why, perhaps he thought my day off would somehow lose him the sale, anyhow as I walked into his office, doctor asked me if I was feeling better.

I might have been feeling great, if I'd known what he was talking about, only my colleague hadn't let me in on his small deception. He'd forgotten to tell me anything about it. It was a long time before I did anything for that colleague again.

At the beginning of a sale, when we're trying hard to build rapport, then a little creative flattery can come in useful. Paying compliments about their house, their children, their tastes, their appearance, may sometimes tax the most vivid imagination, but if you make them feel happy, that's great, there's no harm in that. But lying for the sake of it, is not professional. It's not sense either, because you are sure to be found out.

Respect the customer's right to complain

It's six months since you fitted Pete and Paula Painint'neck's kitchen. It was the finest money could buy. The units went in like a dream, the layout guarantees to save her miles of walking each year, and the decorative effects are so restful

Pete often wakes up halfway through breakfast with his face in the porridge. There's only one minor problem, the manufacturer sent one of the wall units the wrong size, 500mm instead of 600mm.

O.K. so it doesn't look perfect, but at least there's a cupboard there and you have ordered the replacement. There have been delays: first your supplier went on holiday for a month and then when the first replacement came, it was the wrong colour. Not your fault, you don't check replacement confirmations, haven't you enough to do trying to pull in all those site surveys, designs, presentation appointments, not to mention organising installations, re-ordering replacement parts and, most important, making sure you get paid?

You have explained all this to Pete and Paula but they just don't seem to care. You felt it was very rude of Paula to say what she did when the second replacement came. It was the correct colour, you had checked that, it was the correct size, you checked that too, but it wasn't *quite* the right style. Anyone can make a mistake, not you of course, it was your supplier again.

Just then Pete Painint'neck phones: "When are you going to finish my kitchen? It is nearly a year now, since I ordered it."

You: "Hello Mr. Painint'neck, as I told you last week, I have the new unit on order and it should be with you in ten days."

"It better be," he growls, "because if this kitchen is not completed within fourteen days, I am going to my solicitor."

As he puts his phone down you mutter a few words which would not be the subject of the most disreputable graffiti, let alone printed in a book of this quality. In your mind Peter Painint'neck is nothing short of a nuisance. But that is in your mind. In Peter's mind he has a genuine complaint.

There are more than enough reasons why a salesman may have little respect for his customers but genuine complaints are not one of them.

Put yourself in their position and think how you would feel in the circumstances. Would you exaggerate the problems in order to get results, would you involve your solicitor, withhold payment, ask for compensation? If I had a genuine complaint that was slow to be sorted out, I would.

What helps the old reputation, at times like these, is a little extraordinary effort, to let customer know that you are sorry and that you respect their right to complain.

That effort may be a bouquet of flowers for the lady, with a personal note of apology and assurance, or it may be an invitation to dinner, to show that you aren't just dropping them like a hot brick now the job is done.

A bit of extra effort at this point will turn that Lemon into a Peach of a job, and change the: "I wouldn't recommend them to my worst enemy!" into, "We did have one small problem, but they soon sorted it out for us. You won't go wrong buying from them."

A telephone conversation, permeated with the attitude: "Oh no it's that creep again," will do no good. Do all you can to put things right and respect customers' right to complain.

Getting the customer to respect you

Product knowledge is considered by many sales trainers as the main weapon in a salesperson's armoury. Perhaps that is because it is so easy for them to teach! But product knowledge does not sell the goods. It gives you some very well educated prospects, but it won't directly induce them to part with their money.

Where product knowledge is most effective is in its ability to earn you respect, and from that respect – trust. If you know your stuff, your clients will realise, and feel more comfortable in their dealings with you.

One sneaky thing about product knowledge is that, although it comes fairly easy in the beginning – it may be all you know about your job – as the years pass, that knowledge can fade. You may stop using your knowledge, you may feel that, by now, all your prospects know as much as you do about the product. It is this phenomenon which makes it well worth your while to update and refresh your product knowledge at every opportunity.

Do this at trade shows, manufacturer's seminars, in the trade and consumer press, talking to the Rep, or reading the brochures. Don't let the day dawn when your rivals are gaining more respect than you, because they show their product knowledge better.

Knocking the competition

Although you should know your competitors, so that you are able to respond to their competition, you should never mention them. Saying nasty things about competitors lowers your customer's respect; it sounds like sour grapes.

Many a salesman has crossed my threshold, to sell me a product he knows well, but about which I know nothing. Somewhere in the presentation, when I'm being deliberately quiet and awkward, they'll mention the opposition.

I find this very useful. I'm a lazy buyer really. It is especially useful when they tell me about the market leaders and what their particular faults are. Salesman always manages to let you know how much he really respects his main competitor and at these times a pen and paper come in handy.

When this man came in, you only knew of his company, now you know who the good ones are. Never mention the competition.

The mistakes

The time respect is most easily lost is when you commit an error. You may have done ninety per cent of your work correctly then you drop a clanger. The most natural reaction is to get hot under the collar and look hard for someone or something to blame it on. It makes you feel bad to realise you are at fault. None of us likes that.

Well, I have to admit, I made a mistake once. It made such

an impression on me that I went and did it again. Two cardinal sins, making a mistake and then, horror of horrors, making that same mistake again. Well they say to err is human – I have a self inflicted degree in humanities and I'm going for my honours degree!

There are millions of folk who don't make mistakes any more, every one of them laying under a commemorative stone to mark their progression to that achievement. As for you who are still living, then even mistakes can be turned to advantage.

The simple way to do that is to admit them. There is nothing more effective in taking the sting out of a customer's aggressive phone call than saying: "I'm sorry it was my own fault...." Most people will accept that and forgive.

Customers, and salespeople, are all vulnerable human beings; if you present yourself in that light, customers can relate to it and will forgive you. You cannot lose. If you try to flannel your way out of it, you will simply make them madder.

If you do get one who doesn't forgive, well you gave them the chance, if they don't take it forget them. They're not worth worrying about.

Respect yourself
Which leads me on to self respect. A wise person will always listen to another's point of view, he will keep an open mind but will never be convinced to do something he doesn't feel is right.

There is a terrific temptation for a salesperson, who wants to keep the customer sweet, never to say "no". Salesperson feels that he might lose the sale. It has been my experience that even the toughest talking bully will think twice when presented with a firm but smiling refusal to his unreasonable request. And that "Yes men" never command respect, often bringing troubles upon themselves, by appearing to be soft.

Mr. Nasty: "We've paid all this money for the new car, you

don't seriously expect me to pay for those extra accessories do you?"

You – smiling: "Yes please, that will be £225.70 including VAT."

You need never let others bully you. Just say no – you don't even have to explain why – it is enough to smile and say: "I have my own reasons."

We've all been taught to look after our good name above all else, and as advice that's spot-on. Quite a few people, however, forget that they owe that good name to themselves first, and to anyone else a long way second.

You will gain more respect by sticking to your principles, than you will by giving in to unreasonable pressure, (quicker delivery, lower price). If you can pleasantly explain why something is unacceptable to you, you may win the order.

If you go along with something that is wrong, you are bound to fail. If they buy the goods, they'll blame you for the cock-ups and you lose in the end.

Respect your colleagues

Yesterday you were a brilliant salesman, you built so much rapport with the customer, they could hear the bang in the boardroom. But today's prospect doesn't like you. There's only one thing to do, introduce him to your colleague.

There are many situations where someone else can sell when you can't. For instance your female colleague may fare better with some of the lady customers than you do – or with some of the men.

If you sense you're going down like a dose of 'flu, introduce that colleague, but not before you make the customer feel a bit special to get her. Introduce colleague as your senior, as a leading expert in her field. If you are struggling, have enough respect for your colleagues to realise that they may do better.

Personal jealousy often stops you from saying good things about your workmates, yet if overcome, you have a unique and powerful sales-aid which can work to your company's advantage.

Respect your suppliers

There is always a slight temptation, when things do go wrong, to blame it onto the supplier. One of the companies I deal with had a nasty strike a year or two back. Deliveries got well and truly messed about. The temptation at that time was to answer the irate phone calls from impatient customers, with words such as: "They are hopeless – they are really causing us some trouble – they couldn't organise an outing to a brewery."

I know that some of my fellow dealers took that route with their clients. It never works. First of all your customer doesn't care whose fault it is, secondly they pretty soon come to the conclusion that it was you who initially recommended that particular manufacturer, so it's your fault really.

If supplier is causing serious delivery problems it is much better to phone your customers to let them know before they find out the hard way, and to tell them that such delivery problems are most unusual for the supplier and that you have great faith in them to do their best to resolve matters, as they always have done in the past.

Blaming Mr. Supplier will do you no good; if he is no good, dump him. Otherwise back him up at all times.

Respect your employer

We had been invited to Germany, to visit a supplier's factory. The trip was going very well, we were being shown around the works by their British agent. The factory was full to the rafters with manufactured goods. This looked, to me, like a very good omen which just showed how busy they were. I passed this thought on to the agent, who immediately straightened me out.

He told me that they were full up because nothing was going out; there was a scare in the German market about some ingredient used in the manufacture, and sales were static.

Agent took great pleasure in telling me that it was only the British market that was keeping "them" going. That the

Germans were all idiots and without "us," "they" would be in deep financial trouble.

He was trying to gain personal points at the expense of his company and his colleagues. But in doing so he lost my respect. I thought he was disloyal. I wondered why he was working for these people if he felt that way about them. I wondered what he said about me, behind my back!

If you can't respect your employers, you can't have much respect for yourself, or you would not be working for them. A good salesman has a lot of respect, for his suppliers, his workmates, his employer and most of all himself.

The image of Spiv will haunt every salesperson in the world, but it can be laid firmly to rest by the salesperson who can earn his client's respect. Customer will always respect a professional salesperson. That customer will return time and again to the salespeople that they respect. Respect is a vital word in a salesperson's vocabulary, learn it, then learn how to earn it.

9

DEVELOPING THE
MASTER TOUCH

Most people, involved in selling their goods to the retail public, whether those be cars, caravans, replacement windows, holidays, bathrooms, three-piece suites, motorcycles, building extensions, whatever; think that the whole art of selling lies in being able to persuade those customers, who walk into their premises, to buy from them instead of buying from their competitors. And that's not so.

Look at the truly great artists of the past, Van Gogh, Lowry, Picasso and Constable all had to acquire two very distinct skills; first, the technical ability to produce their masterpieces, and second, the creative imagination to dream up their subject matter in the first place. The one without the other is no use.

Many people can paint as well as Van Gogh, Lowry and Picasso, but are unable to match their unique imaginations. It's their imaginations that distinguish the "Masters" from the also-rans.

Selling is no different. To be a top flight salesperson, you need two distinct and different areas of skill. Firstly the techniques and ability to persuade people to buy your goods.

Secondly you need the imagination to find those people in the first place. This is where the excellent stand head and shoulders above the ordinary.

The ordinary sit in the showroom waiting for prospects to

walk through the door, grumbling about the inefficiency of advertising (when they don't), and generally pointing out that the responsibility for finding customers lies with the marketing men.

I suggest that every salesman in the land is an incomplete person if he doesn't do the major part of his own prospecting. And I'm talking about individual salesmen, not the companies for which they work.

It is my belief that being a good sales prospector is 75% of the skill in selling, and prospecting is so easy to do. You just ask as many people as you can find if they are ready to buy your products.

You sell bathrooms. You may be the showroom owner. You may be the departmental manager. You may be the shopfloor employee. You all need bathroom buyers to work with. Let's say you are all capable of converting the same number of prospects into bathroom sales. Let's say that half the people whom you meet in your shop will end up buying from you.

At present you are selling five bathrooms a week, so you are seeing ten prospects a week. All that business is generated from showroom reputation, advertising, manufacturers' promotions and recommendations. There's an awful lot of business that you are missing, you are only doing half a job.

You could be seeing 100 people a week and selling 50 bathrooms, by prospecting for them more effectively.

Let's look at a few ways of doing just that. For the purposes of the exercise, let's say we are retailers selling from this list of products: cars, caravans, replacement windows, holidays, bathrooms, three-piece suites, motor-cycles, building extensions. It works just the same for any other products, but that seems a fair cross-section to me.

Whom do we aim for?
You sell three-piece suites. How many people in your area want your product? Do you think it's 10% of the population, 5%, how many?

Developing the Master Touch

To my way of thinking, that figure is 100%! Everybody in our area wants your goods. If you were giving settees away, they'd all come grabbing. But you are asking for money, so only those who are highly motivated to have a new settee will come in to see you. The others who are completely unmotived to buy, will make do with their old ones.

In a retail situation, only those customers who are dying for it, actually walk in, they are the tip of the iceberg, there's

If we can get our hooks into that floating mass...

an enormous lump of ice, floating just out of our sight. If we can get our hooks into that floating mass and motivate it to surface, our sales figures will soar.

And there is no need to worry about running out of prospects, new ones come into the market daily. You sell caravans: Mrs. Prospect's parents invited the family over to their haven by the sea. For the first time in Mrs. P's life she enjoyed the benefits of a weekend's caravaning. They all had a great time. The previous Friday Mrs. Prospect wasn't even thinking about caravans, now it is Monday and she has decided to buy one.

You sell replacement windows: Mr. Prospect has taken a few days off work, to paint the outside of his house; the first time he tries to scrape some paint off the window a huge lump of rotten wood falls away. On Monday Mr. Prospect was looking for paint to decorate his windows, on Tuesday he is looking for replacement windows.

You sell cars: Young Master Prospect spends the weekend overhauling his old Rover, it is his pride and joy, he loves it. Next Monday morning, on the way to work, a lamp-post jumps off the kerb and completely remodels it. Suddenly Master Prospect is in the car market.

Every day, all over the country there are new people being added to the mass who are motivated enough to want to buy your products. You are a retailer, tied to a showroom or shop, how do you find them? How do you make sure that they know your name? Let's examine a few possibilities.

Tell 'em what you do
The first step is simple, tell everyone you ever meet that you sell cars, that's what your job is and if they want a motor you can help them.

It's a feature of the British reserve that we don't readily tell people what we do for a living, but now you are going to.

If you don't already have some, get some business cards printed. Feature your name, more heavily than that of the company you work for, these cards are going to work for you personally. To increase your commission and through that, your company's turnover.

If the company won't supply you with cards, buy your own and then distribute them. Most companies I know have business cards printed for their salespeople who give away 10–15 a week maximum. Make sure you give away that number every day, *minimum*.

Give them to everyone you meet both in your business and

social life. Your doctor, his receptionist, your dentist, the policeman who stopped you for speeding, the milkman, postman, grocer, the lads down the pub, the landlord, the hairdresser, the vicar, verger, choir master. District councillor, your neighbour, midwife, the dustbin men, the chap standing next to you on the football terraces.

All you need to do is pass a few pleasantries with them and end up by saying: "By the way I sell Nisda cars. Here's my card, if ever you're looking for a sound set of wheels come and see me. I'll look after you."

Mail-outs

Another good use for personal business cards, to bring *you* sales, is accompanying mail-outs.

If you are selling a product where repeat business is likely, caravans, holidays, cars, etc, your mail-out is designed to keep your name in front of your potential customers, and to remind them that you exist, so that when they become motivated to buy the products that you sell, they know where to come.

If you are selling something where repeat business is unlikely, replacement windows, bathrooms, building extensions, etc., then the mail-out technique is slightly different.

It is 'the numbers game', you are batting much more in the dark, posting off, on a random basis, a coloured brochure that describes your goods, with a company compliments slip and your personal business card. On the compliments slip simply write a short message, say: "Can we quote for your new – replacement windows – fitted kitchen – home extension – carpets – decorating – garden shed? Please phone me on 123654."

The numbers are vastly improved if you can be sure the people you are mailing to have some need for your goods or service. For instance anyone applying for planning permission to build or improve their home is likely to want one of, if not all of, the products in that list. You can find out who

is applying for such permission through visiting the local
council offices where such information is open to examination

In fact these days there are firms who exist by selling lists of
those applying for building permission.

Others who would be interested in buying our list of
products are those who are moving house. You can find out
who they are by keeping an eye on the homes for sale notices
in the paper, in estate agents' windows and in the county
magazine; all are sources of names for our mailing list.

Woo the ladies

When using mailing lists that are open to all, the chances that
you are the only one sending mail-outs will be pretty slim, so
you need to ensure that the envelope gets opened and your
note gets read. The best way to get the envelope opened is to
handwrite the name and address.

I always open handwritten envelopes before I tackle the
typed ones. If the writer has addressed his letter with his own
fair biro, the chances are that it's good news, either a message
from a friend who is keeping in touch, or, in a business
situation, it is a payment from a customer.

If the envelope is typewritten then it's either a bill, or it is
from someone wanting to sell me something!

So to dodge the waste bin, address envelopes by hand. At
the risk of leaving myself open to criticism, I'm going to
suggest something now which is distinctly sexist. Address
your envelope to Mrs. Prospect. She probably receives far less
mail than her husband and because it is handwritten she
knows it isn't from a mail-order catalogue, *Readers Digest*,
Which, or another of the "send it back and go in the prize-
draw", brigade. So she will be pleased to open it. And don't
send your mail-outs in buff envelopes, all businesses use buff
envelopes. Buy some white ones, they're still relatively cheap.
If you want to be really sure she opens the mail, and the
budget allows it, use coloured ones.

When you know the address but not the names, don't put

"The Occupier", put "The Lady of the House". It shows more flair, and it works better.

Making time

"Hold on," you may be saying. "Where am I going to get the time to send off mail-shots?" Good question and I've got a good answer. Don't make a big thing out of it. If you can post out ten envelopes every day, then all that's going to cost you is around 20 minutes of your time. I do mine first thing every morning just before I sift through the post and check the diary. But then I always was a creature of comfortable routines.

The nice thing about mail-outs is that they can be useful little time-fillers to be done every time a spare five minutes comes along. Make yourself a strong rule though. You don't go home unless the postman has ten of your business cards winging toward a potential customer's mail-box. Ten a day is 50 a week and if you get one or two of them in to see you, then you're on your way.

If you still don't think you've got the time for any of these prospecting methods, concentrate your mind on the amount of time that can be wasted during a day.

We only have eight hours, and a typical morning can start with that cup of coffee, the chat with your colleagues about last night's snooker match or how sexy your favourite film actor looked in the film on the BBC.

Then out come the holiday snaps or the pictures of the new baby and someone remembers a joke they had been told by Robert the representative yesterday and all of a sudden it's time for elevenses.

O.K. so that's not you but I bet this is. Cup of coffee in hand you sit down at the desk and start to file away the price lists that came yesterday.

The phone rings, someone wants to know if you want to buy some advertising, you tell them that the advertising budget is pre-planned for the next six months and you don't want to talk to them, twenty minutes and a lot of "we don't want any's," later, you hang up and start again on your job.

The phone rings. The chap from stores wants to know if he should order a thousand of your least popular items because a salesman is pestering him, and "will you have a word with him?" You say no but it's too late. And fifteen minutes later you start again on your price lists.

And then the phone rings, it's your darling spouse wanting to know if you will be able to take junior miss to her gymnastics class. Ten minutes later you are a little warm under the collar and you start again.

The phone rings. . . .

That's almost 13% of your day gone and not a penny earned. Perhaps you used not to mind these little inter-ruptions, but you will do now.

Ring their bell

Another effective tool for finding new prospects is the telephone. We can't get out of the shop to call on possible customers so let's do it on the phone. Cold calling is possibly the most effective way of being in touch with the right customer, at the right time. The most effective and the least popular.

It's the least popular because we all *know* that whoever picks up the receiver at the other end, is going to waltz through our earpiece and maim us for life, and if they don't do that, they are going to say NO!

Those who extol the virtues of positive thinking may tell us to approach each and every phone call we make with the positive belief that the call will result in a sale. In reality that will only happen, at best, about five times in every hundred. It is important in cold calling, on the phone, to keep this sense of realism in mind.

If you dial with the positive expectation that most of your prospects are going to say "no," then, when that odd one does say "yes," you'll be like a dog with two tails. Every time you make a call remember one thing, you can't possibly lose anything. You had nothing when you picked the phone up and not even the tax man can take that away from you!

If you don't like cold prospecting, and the results are very low, why should you do it? You could be having a peaceful time, waiting for customer to come in, reading your newspaper, drinking your beverages, but if you do that you won't make any money. If you cold call instead, you will make money. And everyone wants to make money; if you didn't, you wouldn't have suffered the trauma of dragging your reluctant body out of bed in the morning.

It is a fact in business that most "recommends" walk in immediately after an advertising campaign. No-one saw the advert, no-one will have received a mail-out, no-one will have had one of your phone calls, yet in they come.

As soon as you stop prospecting, they stop coming. The "recommends" dry up. All of which goes to prove the old adage: "You don't ask, you won't get."

If you make cold calls on the telephone you'll make more money. It may not flow in like a pools win, but steadily and surely the money will come. When I first heard this idea put forward, it was suggested that the best way to get real results was to make six calls per hour until you die.

Death came quickly and cleanly. By lunch-time on the first day the curly cord and my epiglottis had made arrangements to hang up permanently. Every ten minutes is over the top; you may enjoy a lunch of fish and chips, but if someone gives you a well fried blue whale to eat, you're going to lose some enthusiasm for sea-food.

I finished up with a quota of one call every two hours, four a day, but even that was hard going, because the other thing my mentor said was that I had to have a script. For this script to work it had to lull the customer into a false sense of no obligation – we just happened to have someone working their area that day, so it was no trouble.

So off I dialled, searching furiously for my script, hidden

under all the papers on my desk. Just in time I find it: "Hello, Mrs. Prospect?" "Yes."

Me: "Ah, Mrs. Prospect. Mrs. Prospect I'm phoning on behalf of the Bettathanmost Home Improvement Centre of Hope Valley. The reason I'm calling you this evening, Mrs. Prospect, is that we have a surveyor in your area who is giving advice on home improvements and offering a free, no-obligation design service. Could this be of any help to you Mrs. Prospect?"

I thought I was doing a great job, such a subtle introduction to our wares.

Then she'd say something like: "What did you say?" And I'd be in trouble. Either I'd buried the script again or by the time I'd repeated that lot, she'd be snoring. Pretty soon I'd gone past the time my next call was due and she's still saying things like: "I'll fetch my husband. Who did you say you were? I don't live here really it's my daughter-in-law you want."

Something had to give. It's no good making one call every two hours if you're on the phone for three hours at a time.

So I changed things. All I really wanted to know was, does this person want to buy my goods. So I asked that instead.

Me: "Hello, Mrs. Prospect?"

Her: "Yes."

Me: "Have you completed the plans for your home improvements yet?"

The question is such a surprise to our prospect that more often than not she answers without hestitation: "We're not doing any home improvements."

So now I know, this person does not want to buy my goods. I simply say: "O.K. goodbye." And put the phone down. Don't linger. You haven't wasted time on unnecessary pleasantries, you haven't even told her your name.

Let's try some more.

US: "Hello, Mr. Pullit?"

HIM: "Yes, who is it?"

US: "Have you bought your new caravan yet?"

HIM: "No as a matter of fact I don't like caravans."

US: "Thank you. Goodbye."

Direct questions are likely to bring out direct answers. Dial another.

US: "Hello, Mrs. Sailaway?"

HER: "Yes."

US: "Have you booked your next holiday yet."

HER: "Yes as a matter of fact we go next month, who wants to know?"

US: "Thank you. Goodbye."

We ask the questions, we're not in it for the conversation. It may seem discourteous but we haven't the time to waste chatting. Let's try again.

US: "Hello. Mr. Bodgit?"

HIM: "Yes."

US: "Have you bought your replacement windows yet?"

HIM: "Well, how did you know I needed new windows. I only found out they were rotten this morning."

Eureka! You've found somebody who wants to buy. You didn't need a script, you haven't taken but a minute or two, and if he takes umbrage at you calling he doesn't know whom to swipe at.

It's the variety of the answers that makes this form of phone canvassing so much fun. You can't know what they are going to reply but because you use such a direct question you are likely to get a direct answer.

That may be: "I don't want a new car. – Who wants to know? – (dead silence) – Get off the line you pervert."

Or it just might be: "How did you know I wanted to put in a new tennis court?" Bingo, you have caught a prospect.

Now you need to know what to say, and that's easy. The right words come flooding into mind as soon as you ring off, they always do. Meanwhile you have a prospect to answer and no-one can tell you what to say. All I can tell you is the more you call, the easier it is to find the right answers to the questions they throw back at you.

If you do find yourself in the position of only being able to say: "errrrr. I ummm." Ring off. You know his number, you know he's a possible customer. When you've thought out what to do you can always phone back.

Can I honestly suggest that these three simple methods: telling everyone what you sell, mail-outs and telephone canvassing, will bring you in more prospects every week? Can I promise you that when your colleagues are standing around kicking their heels and moaning about the shop advertising not being effective, you will be talking to people who have come in just to see you? Yes I Can.

10

SETTING THE
APPOINTMENT

Hymie Hummalong and Dennis Drudge work for the same
company, selling corn plasters. They work the chemist shops.
Chemists tend to be dour folk, professional people who are
also busy shopkeepers. Like many other business people,
chemists do not relish time spent with salesmen, especially
salesmen calling on them for the first time, salesmen whom
they do not know.

The cold call
Dennis tries to set his initial appointments like this: "I'm
Dennis Drudge from Dryitup and Ddroppoff, do you sell our
Corn Plasters?"

"I don't know young man, I've only come in to buy some
laxative. You want Mr. Pharmacist."

Dennis: "Excuse me, are you Mr. Pharmacist?"

Mr. P.: "Just a moment young man, I'm preparing a
potion. Can Mrs. P. help?"

Dennis: "Oh yes. Hello Mrs. Pharmacist. My name is
Dennis Drudge from Dryitup and Ddroppoff, our cornplasters are made of the toughest rubber, have ergonomically
designed corn compounds and come in three colours."

Mrs. P.: "Just move aside young man, it is morning surgery
time, we are very busy."

Dennis stands around for 20 minutes until the chemist

begins to feel that he is making the place look untidy and says:
"Now then young man what can I do for you?"

"My name is Dennis Drudge from Dryitup and Ddroppoff,
do you sell our cornplasters?"

Mr. P.: "Oh, you're a rep, I haven't got time to talk to you
just now. Goodbye."

Dennis walked in unannounced and tried to sell his goods
in one fell swoop. Great if it had worked. But it didn't; it
didn't work a lot of times for Dennis. He was a hard worker
though, he kept slogging away. At every month end he would
proudly show his sales manager that he did twice as many
calls, every day, as his colleague, Hymie.

Hymie tackled it this way:

In the chemist's window is a little notice, it gives the times
of the local doctor's surgery – 8.45 am to 10.45 am – 4 pm to 6
pm. Hymie has a copy of these times in his notebook, for
every chemist on his patch. He arrives at chemists after the
morning rush has finished.

Behind the counter, proudly displayed for all to see, is the
chemist's qualification certificate. It gives his name, and tells
Hymie how long he's been in practice.

Hymie begins his quest for an appointment in stages, the
first stage goes like this: "Hello Mr. Pharmacist, I can see that
you are busy, and I don't want to take up any of your valuable
time just now. When would you be able to spare me a couple
of minutes to answer a simple question?"

Hymie hasn't gone in to sell the chemist any corn plasters,
his objective this time is to sell Mr. Pharmacist the idea of
setting an appointment. The old chemist probably knows
this, but because Hymie's approach has taken account of his
limited time, because it is polite, and because he can put it off
until a time comfortably into the future, Mr. Pharmacist is
likely to answer favourably.

More likely than not, he'll say: "Well young man I can
spare time to answer one question right now, but only two
minutes mind."

Warming the call up

Hymie now has his opportunity to sell the appointment, and he needs to say something that will immediately catch the old alchemist's interest, perhaps: "I have been able to help a number of others in the pharmaceutical trade make up to 80% more money out of their surgical appliance sales. At this point, I can't say for definite that I can do the same for you, but if you could spend ten minutes or so with me to answer one or two very simple questions, we'll soon find out. When could we do that, later on this afternoon, or early tomorrow morning?"

Questions which begin with a short statement, telling the prospect that he will have more pounds and pennies in his hot little palm, will cause him to think: "Hey this sounds interesting, I'll talk to this guy." And Hymie has gained a degree of control. He has also set his appointment.

Setting an appointment is a sale, like any other, so go for a definite close. If he's in the market for your products, he'll allow you to set a time. A time which he has committed himself to and which he is highly unlikely to cancel.

If he isn't interested, he'll probably reply: "I order my cornplasters direct, and I can't afford to waste my time talking to you."

If he does, simply hand him a card, ask him to contact you if ever you can be of any help to him, say farewell and go. But don't forget him. You have a serious job of wooing to do, including sending him mail-outs, dropping in and asking if you can be of any help, inviting him to corn plaster application demonstration buffets, thinking up any possible reason for phoning him up to speak to him, and generally letting him know that you like him, and are still around selling corn plasters.

I can guarantee that if you take this approach, you will be one of very few who are properly trying to set real selling appointments. So many salespeople are happy simply showing their face. They hate cold calls. They just *know* they don't work.

This is the best reason of all for doing them. There is nothing which will make you more perfect in your job than practice, and there is nothing that gives salespeople better practice than cold calling. You have never seen your new prospects before, you don't know what they are like or what they are likely to say.

Dealing with these unknowns will keep your wits sharp and your mind alert. If you look on cold calling as a form of training, that your competitors do not do, then the thought of getting one up on the competition can make this exercise great fun, and turn those odd successes, where you actually go away with a sale, into euphoric experiences.

With cold calling you have all to gain and absolutely nothing to lose. You walk in there with nothing, you will come out with a bit more experience and perhaps an order. What more could you want?

A telephone appointment

Most salespeople, who face the task of phoning around, to try and set sales appointments, are so unthrilled by the idea that the only way they can do it is by "getting it over with" as quickly as possible. They slope into their office, block everything else out of their minds, pick up the dreaded device and start dialling before they can find something more comfortable to do. They don't even consider their sales strategy.

To master the phone appointment, we all should have a clear understanding of what we wish to achieve, just as we should in a toe-to-toe situation. Firstly we need to ask ourselves a question: Whom should I "sell" the idea of an appointment to? Who, within the organisation, will benefit most from buying my wares or my services?

Let's say you sell advertising. Finding out who you should talk to is as easy as asking the receptionist: "Before you put me through, could you tell me please – Who looks after your advertising? – Who is in charge of your advertising? – Who is responsible for buying advertising?"

I know that some receptionists are recruited from the school for the cretinous, deaf or indifferent, before they are allowed on the blower and your request will often be met by the silence of the "hold" button, or a mind sharpening: "You wo-o-ot?" But you've got to try.

If she can speak intelligibly, try and acquire the full name of your prospect. Not just Miss Graphicbuyer but Geraldine Graphicbuyer. Learning the Christian name of your prospect comes in very useful when you have to circumnavigate a wary secretary whose purpose in life is to protect "the boss" from folk like you.

I don't go in for flaunting first names with the prospect themselves, not before a good relationship has been built up. It can easily antagonise.

Here we go on our phone call to try and set an appointment with Miss Graphicbuyer.

Receptionist: "Lacy Fabrics."

Us: "Hello, Geraldine Graphicbuyer please." Receptionist is our first target and the use of our prospect's Christian name sounds as if we know them personally.

Receptionist: "I'll put you through to her secretary." Or more likely, she'll put you straight through.

Secretary: "Miss Graphicbuyer's office, who's speaking please?" A great many secretaries act as a screen to their busy boss, so now we need to minimise the effectiveness of that screen.

Us: "Oh, hello, is Geraldine in?" Go in with a direct question, it demands a direct answer, you may just get: "Yes I'll put you through." More likely though.

Secretary: "One moment, I'll find out for you. May I ask who is speaking please?"

Us: "Stephanie Spaceseller from the FashionMakers Monthly."

This secretary is not going to be by-passed that easily:

"Could you tell me what it's about please?"

The last thing you want is to sell an appointment to a secretary who cannot make the decision you require. If you can make your next sentence sound as if it will be of great benefit to her boss, and perhaps make it sound technical, to bamboozle her a little, she will put you through – just in case it is important.

Us: "I wanted to discuss the promotional editorial with Geraldine, to maximise the P.R. launch of your autumn ranges. She is still in charge of marketing isn't she?"

Secretary: "Yes she is."

Us: "Smashing, can I speak to her?"

You deserve to be through, but it doesn't always work like that. And sure enough, this time it doesn't. It's no good muttering dark oaths under your breath, you've got to get down and get thinkin'; use the old imagination.

If secretary is going to see whether Miss GraphicBuyer is interested in talking to you, it will help your cause if she presents your case well. Start off by making a friend, ask her her name, ask her a few questions about herself, have a joke. Make her your ally. Develop rapport.

Ask her opinion as to the best ways to present your wares to her boss. If you're still not getting through, don't give up, keep phoning secretary. Sooner or later this conversation will take place.

Secretary to boss: "You've just got to speak to Stephanie Spaceseller, she must have called you eight or nine times. I don't know what to say to her any more. She sounds ever so nice, will *you* have a word with her?"

Let's say you've drawn a really anti-social one though. An old Bustard. A secretary who hates advertising salespeople. Is there anything else you can do? Of course there is!

You could call after normal working hours. Bosses often stay late, to get a bit of peace and quiet, without their secretaries. Or you could call when secretary goes to lunch. If you cannot get past her, try going around.

If you cannot get past her, try going around.

Your competition may even be sneaky enough to find out when "the wall" goes on holiday. Be sneaky first.

Even when our telephone appointment has been successfully set you may not get to pass Go. How many times have you turned up, at the appointed time, only to find out that prospect is not there? It happens to salespeople time and time again, and it is as well to bear this possibility in mind when you make the appointment.

You need to sell as much commitment into that time as you possibly can. Let your prospective customer know that you have set that time aside, especially for him, out of your busy schedule, or that you are coming a long way specially, or whatever.

The subtlest way to tell him is to set definite times which are slightly out of the norm, say 11.35 or 3.15, avoid the o'clocks and half-pasts and hint at a busy schedule. (Forget 11 am and 2 pm, salesman's rush hour, let the others pester him at those old favourites.)

Back up this busy schedule theme by telling your prospect that you have planned to be at a definite destination before you visit him and at another appointment afterwards, so his appointment with you is part of a larger plan.

If the first time that you suggest is inconvenient then so much the better. If for instance an afternoon appointment is inconvenient for your prospect, but a morning appointment is not, tell him that by rearranging your morning appointment or rescheduling your route and changing your overnight arrangements, you can accommodate him. It will be a hard man who breaks an appointment after all that commitment by you.

When you have to burn rubber to get before your customers, don't let that travel and appointment time be taken lightly. And remember, if you really want to double your earnings, the best way is to double your presentation appointments. If you want to do it you can.

11

THE ABC OF SELLING

Selling has been called many things: the art of persuading the customer to buy your goods instead of someone else's. The art of making friends, who buy your goods willingly, etc., etc.

To me selling is the art of making a living and if we can keep it as simple as ABC we will probably find that task takes up less of our time and leaves us free to indulge in the art of enjoying our lives and families.

Of course it isn't that simple, or I'd have retired to Cannes by now. The whole spectrum that makes up a sale looks something like this:-

*PROSPECTING.	Looking for customers.
*QUALIFYING.	The prospects you have found.
*PRESENTING.	Your wares to a qualified prospect.
*DEMONSTRATING.	To prove that your goods work.
*ANSWERING OBJECTIONS.	To clear the way for agreement.
*CLOSING.	Gaining agreement to buy.
*FOLLOW-UP.	Keeping customer sweet for repeat business.

It is not a very long list, but some salespeople find it very difficult to adhere to. They are the amateurs.

Amateur

Amateurs expect others to provide them with prospects, they don't bother qualifying their customers to find out how serious they are. It seems easier to plug on and waste time, rather than to ask a few pertinent questions to see how the land really lies.

They rush through the presentation with no real plan of action nor any idea of what they should be achieving. These folk are easily recognised by their bad manners and the number of their prospects who go away: "to think about it."

Amateur is often asked questions about the product that he cannot answer. When it comes to demonstrating the benefits of his product, he often finds that the factory has supplied him with one that doesn't quite work. Amateur makes a lot of excuses, not for himself you understand. Amateur is surrounded by idiots but never looks in a mirror!

Amateur sees his customer's objections as a personal attack on his integrity which must be defended at all costs. He will argue his point of view to the bitter end secure in the knowledge that it is right. Either that or he is so frightened of losing the sale that he will agree with anything customer says.

Amateur does not close sales; his customers buy off him. They are heard asking questions such as: "Where do we go from here then?" and, "How soon could we have it delivered?" But Amateur doesn't listen. He hasn't finished telling them how much more he knows about his product than they do. He rarely shuts up long enough to hear them ask the all-important question: "Whom do I make the cheque payable to?"

Ask Amateur what follow-up is and he'll tell you that it is making sure that the person he has just taken money off leaves the building. Once they have gone, he forgets them. All he can expect from them now is complaints that the product does not do what he said it would, that it has broken down, that the final bill is much higher than they expected. Amateur hates customers, they are nothing but trouble.

Amateur is someone who holds completely the wrong attitude to be selling for a living, he does the profession nothing but harm. I have often had younger salespeople say to me that they just made a terrible mistake and that they do not feel very professional because of it. I have to sympathise with them, because I made all the same mistakes myself ten years ago. And then again eight years ago – six – four – two years ago and still will be in ten years' time.

It's easy to see why I don't believe that making mistakes means you are an amateur.

Be your own best customer

Here are a few ideas to ponder which may make you a more professional person.

Before you start trying to sell your product, sell yourself first. You will never *persuade* people to buy your product if they haven't bought you first. They need to like you, to trust you and to respect you; the first words you say to them should be directed towards achieving that aim.

You will never pick up repeat business if you sell rubbish. In politics they may be able to fool some of the people all of the time and all of the people some of the time. But then people don't expect much of politicians. In selling, if you fool any one of the people just one time it will cost you. Not only will "fool" never pass your portals again, he will make sure that none of his friends or acquaintances comes to see you either.

You will be surprised just how many people one "conned" customer knows. Each one of those acquaintances could have been a referral, so be careful what you sell. Be your own best customer. Try out the brands you sell, test them, particularly the after-sales service. It's one thing to earn yourself a bad reputation. Don't let your supplier do it for you. Friends like that you do not need.

Every now and again put yourself in your customer's shoes. If you are managing a sales team, or several branches

Every now and again put yourself in your customer's shoes.

of a retail outlet, take time to see what goes on at shop floor
level. Visit old customers personally to make sure they still
love your product and service. Show them that you still love
them. You may get a share of flak. But flak that you know
about won't shoot you down.

Don't hide yourself away behind things. Many of the other
professions, medical people, solicitors, accountants, computer people, camouflage themselves behind a complicated
language which only certain other members of their
profession can comprehend.

Unless you are selling neurosurgical litigative debtor
ledger roms, then complicated terminology will only serve to
confuse. Professional salespeople's customers are never
confused about what they are buying.

ABCs

And what about you? Some days, when the sun is shining, all
your customers can say is: "Yes please!" Then the job of
salesperson is like falling off a log. However not every day is

like that. There are those days when even the most
professional amongst us demonstrates all the attributes of the
worst amateur.

Like the time when milkman left you that extra pot of
cream and wife's favourite yoghurt; when the mother of your
children was in a blissfully happy mood. You often wondered
why youngest son had blond hair while all your relatives were
red heads. This particular morning the penny dropped.

This day you got out of bed five minutes early, just in time
to see wife floating off into the dawn on a cartful of gold tops.
Eloping forever to a life of strawberry yoghurt and rattling
crates. All you have left is a mortgage and four mouths to
feed.

Are you depressed? Are you going out to work full of the
joys of spring and with creative energy bursting from every

... ready to sell hair gel to a bald man?

pore, ready to sell hair gel to a bald man? You are?? You've
got a girlfriend lined up, haven't you?

Well, just in case you haven't, let's look at a technique that
is really simple to remember on those bad days when your

mind is full of other things, when selling is hard. Something
that we all learned in those bygone times of childhood, our
ABC.

If you can master these three little letters, you will pick up
commission cheques, even on the dark days when you're
wishing you were in an easier profession, like school teaching
or road sweeping, or brain surgery for instance. A is for
advantage, B for benefit and C for commitment.

Advantage: is an interesting feature of your particular
product which will be an advantage to *you* when it comes to
describing the product to a prospect. A feature which gives
you something to talk about. This feature is always most
powerful if it is something which is unique to your company.
It is well worthwhile compiling a list of the features of your
product or service which are not available to your
competitors, they are the features which you should sell first,
the most obvious unique feature being you.

Vacuum cleaner salesman to housewife: "When you take
this cleaner home with you, not only do you get the turbo
brush head, the ecologically re-cycled dust bags and the cable
recoil system. Guaranteed to ensure that your home is really
clean. Not only do you get all these things, you get me! If at
any time in the future you have any worries with this
particular machine just pick up the phone and ask for me, I'll
be delighted to hear from you. Will you do that?"

Benefit: is what is in it for the customer. How that
interesting feature turns into a direct benefit for them. Their
reason to buy.

Commitment: is the customer's agreement that the feature
you have described will be of benefit to him.

You've probably remembered the saying: "Don't sell the
feature, sell the benefit – Don't sell the steak, sell the sizzle."
Well we are going to take it one step further.

Only sell the feature when it is accompanied by a benefit,
only sell the benefit when it is accompanied by a
commitment.

It will do you no good selling the sizzle from a Fillet Steak if your customers are vegetarians. They won't give you any commitment.

Let's have a short look at a few ABCs:

Car salesman to customer: (A) The Volvo has a very strong passenger compartment, (B) this means that your whole family will be so much safer on the roads. (C) How much does that mean to you?

Kitchen designer to Mrs. Public: (A) This layout gives you almost twice the storage that you have at present, (B) which means that you will be able to find a home for all those items that are filling your worktops and so will keep your kitchen so much tidier. (C) Wouldn't you just love to have an uncluttered kitchen?

Manufacturer to dealer: (A) Our terms give you a discount of 65% whilst still maintaining competitive retail prices. (B) You can just see what a difference margins like this will make to your gross profits, (C) can't you?

Jewellery salesman to house-husband: (A) This gold chain is unique to us, and we have only had ten commissioned. (B) This means that your wife will be the only one amongst her friends with such a lovely necklace. (C) I'm sure she will love you for giving her such a unique gift, aren't you sure too?

Lorry spares salesman to transport manager: (A) These bearings are self-lubricating; they will never wear out, (B) which means that you will never have a truck off the road with worn wheel bearings, giving them more running time in which to create greater profits. (C) An increase in profit is something we all want. Don't you agree?

Once you've mastered your ABC you can relax in the knowledge that you can face the rigours no matter what. You can develop into a star. Be bigger than your product. Flow with an enthusiasm that is impossible to ignore, entertain your customers with an outgoing personality. Enjoy every moment of what you do, that's salesmanship. Sorry ladies, that's salespersonship.

12

OPENING THE SALE

Opening the sale is just as important as closing, yet so many salespeople allow their customers to wander around the showrooms, with no direction, and actually wait until customer approaches and asks if they can "please buy something." Picture this.

Boy, is business slow. It's halfway through Wednesday morning, on one of those drizzly days designed to render the liveliest of spirits lethargic. Your mood for the day is set by the discovery that last night's rain has found its way under the door and has taken up residence in that new pile of brochures, delivered only yesterday after an agonising delay of around three months. They're ruined.

You slouch off to kick the showroom cat and make yourself a cup of coffee. How can you sell anything without proper brochures? It takes you the best part of an hour to separate and dry them all out.

Only last week your boss sent you to a seminar designed to help you close every sale going. You learnt 55 unique and original closes.

Boss has left you in no doubt that the shop's turnover figures are close to the point where someone is going to get fired. You! She has urged you to take note of that fact and to do better.

This couple, dripping quietly over the pile of wrinkled leaflets, are your opportunity to do just that. Fifty-five closes, what chance do they stand?

You yawn, march purposefully towards them wearing your concern in the worry lines on your brow. Too late, you remember to smile, they avert their eyes and turn away, glancing quickly over your award-winning display of merchandise.

"Can I help you?" You have to raise your voice a little, it's not easy addressing the back of someone's head.

It's not easy addressing the back of someone's head.

"No thank you. We're just looking." The shop fluorescents show up the mismatch between his natural hair and the toupee, where they join just above the nape in his neck.

"Would you like some leaflets?" You try to sound bright but...

"No thank you. Goodbye!"

This is just not right. They haven't been in the shop long enough for you to test any of those new demon closes, only long enough, in fact, for the bruised cat to put his territorial scent mark on your coffee mug! You promise yourself to find a job where you don't have to work with animals and the general public.

So what should you have said? Did I tell you that I went to a sales seminar once? Well this one concentrated on *opening* the sale. The speaker told us that to open a sale, we should never say: "Can I help you?" Because our customers will always say: "No thank you, I'm just looking." That's the rule, works every time.

Instead, the seminar man said that a sale should be opened with:

"*How* may I help you?"

The idea being that any question starting with How, What, Where, Why, When and Who cannot be answered with a Yes or No.

This seemed highly logical so I tried it.

Me: "How may I help you?"

Customer: "We are just looking thank you."

You see, the trouble with most customers is that they don't bother to learn their lines properly. It's they who should go to all these seminars, not us!

Other favourite answers to the "How may I help" question have been:

"No." – "By leaving us alone." – "You can't." – "What time is it?" and "Lend us a fiver."

Let's smash a few myths. Let me suggest that you open all your sales the same way. Not with any words; you start with a smile, the brightest one you've got. Practise 'til it reaches from ear to ear and most of all until you mean it. Very few people will be able to stop themselves from smiling back at you, but one or two will. You will see that old familiar scowl that means: "Clear off, you're not going to trick me into buying something."

But, so far, in opening this sale, you've said nowt. Now you're going to clear the scowl with: "Hello." Followed by a loud silence.

Give them the chance to return your greeting. Believe it or not this is usually enough to start clients talking to you about what they want. It can't be this easy, can it? It is.

Make 'em laugh

The first objective, when opening your sale, is to develop rapport with the prospective customer – get them to buy you first, remember. By far the most effective way to make friends is to let your customers know that you like them. And the way to let them know that you like them is by showing an interest in them.

Start by encouraging them to talk about the subject which interests them most – themselves – and show your interest by listening attentively to what they say.

The most successful way to set the ball rolling is by paying them a personal compliment and then asking them about the subject of that compliment. Forget the goods to be sold for a moment, concentrate on selling yourself to them. On persuading them to like you.

And if you get them laughing, you've cracked it.

A great many salespeople introduce themselves to their customers by babbling away about themselves and what they have got. "I've been in the lighting business for twenty-five years, I've sold chandeliers to the Crowned Heads of Europe and spare tubes to the Hollywood Greats. I've got lamps on offer from every country on the globe and ranging in price from £2.50 to £25,000 .. blah .. blah .. blah." So what? Who cares? Not customer that's for sure.

But this chap thinks that his ears are there to hook his spectacles round. Let the poor customer try and dent his ego exposition with a question and he simply raises his voice a few decibels. He thinks of something else to impress them with and by the time he's finished he is shouting fit to blow the showroom lights out.

Customers don't want to be shouted at. Instead of shouting, listen, as quietly as you can.

Dale Carnegie said: "You can make more friends in two months by becoming really interested in other people, than you can in two years by trying to get other people interested in you."

Similarly, you can develop more rapport in two minutes listening with genuine interest, to your customers, than you can in two hours telling them about yourself and your products.

What has all this to do with opening our sales? OK, here we go to open a wet Wednesday's sale.

Us – Smile.

Them – Smile back.

Us – "Hello." Pause.

Them – 'Cripes it's gone quiet.' "Hello."

Us – "Excuse me for saying so, but that is a lovely perfume you are wearing, what is it?"

They will tell you, and you have an opening, but don't overdo it, one compliment is enough, then get down to the task in hand.

The go-pedal statement

You sell gas appliances. Mr. and Mrs. Customer have just told you that they have recently moved house and their new abode has no central heating. They don't know whether to have a gas fired boiler, or electric storage heaters.

To open up this sale properly, you need a statement that's going to catch their attention. An initial benefits statement. Something which tells them how much better your ideas will be for them and then the advantages of your specific product or services over others. Something that gets them listening. A go-pedal statement.

"I can really save you some money here!" is a great go-pedal statement. Another one is: "Oh, I know just the thing you're looking for." These are phrases, designed to get customers pricking their ears up and have to be followed by a statement that will interest them. It's no good getting them to listen if what you say is a disappointment; that only serves to bore them rigid.

Gas salesman again: "What have been of enormous interest to so many of our other customers are the new, heat-exchanger gas boilers, and the great thing about them is that they warm up your house quicker, and cost less than any other form of heating. Plus, you can have a separately heated hot water tank which gives baths full of steaming hot water, without the need to fire up the central heating boiler on warm days. Saves even more money! Does that interest you?"

A go-pedal statement that catches their attention starts the ball rolling. And if the first five minutes of our sale go smoothly, we are well on the road to a satisfied customer.

Contradicting myself

Having said all this I must admit that my favourite opening tactic is to ask the question: "Can I help you?"

That large intake of breath is all the sales trainers in the country sucking in before spouting out that I don't know what I'm talking about. But I've got news for them, I do.

The reason I favour this question is that you know what's coming next, either you get: "Yes please. We are looking to replace our old music centre with a stacking stereo system." In which case you're on your way.

Or you will get that old perennial: "No thanks we're just looking."

We knew it was coming didn't we? We've been there before haven't we? We are ready, with: "Fine, I won't pester you, just tell me the kind of thing you are looking for and I'll show you where to find it."

Customer: "We want to look at stereo units."

Us, and here comes the go-pedal statement: "Great. We have something really special in stereos! Just listen to this new Bang and Wallop compact disc player. The clarity of sound is nectar to even the most discerning ear, and the discs will never deteriorate, no matter how they are handled. They are so hi-tech you'll need the shop steps to reach them. Let me show you." They may not be in the market for a compact disc player, but while you are showing them, you can start to qualify which market they are in.

Qualifying

Qualifying sales prospects is probably one of the most feared techniques in selling. What if you qualify them so well that you know they can't afford to buy your wares? Isn't it better to present and hope? No, of course it isn't, you need to know that the customer can afford to buy what you are selling, just as you need to be sure they want your product and aren't just browsers. But the operative word is qualifying, not disqualifying, and the idea is that we do end up selling them something. We just want to find out what.

There is nothing magical about qualifying, and the time to gather in this information is just before you begin your presentation proper, and the method to use is . . . you've guessed it . . . asking questions.

Music shop salesman: "Is it to be a present for another member of the family, or is it for your own enjoyment, because if it is, we have some really top quality equipment, specially designed for music lovers, in the back room. Would you like me to show you?"

Customer: "Oh yes please, we want to treat ourselves to the best equipment we can afford."

Salesman: "Tell me how much you were thinking of spending?"

Customer: "About £450."

Salesman: "Fine, and did you want to pay cash, or will you take advantage of our excellent two years credit scheme?"

The answers to these questions tell you what to recommend and how to gear your presentation. £450 is probably too low for your better quality equipment, in which case the first thing that you sell to them is you. The second thing you sell is your finance scheme and the last thing you sell are the goods. To a great many customers, an extra £10 per month does not sound as bad as £690.

Open your sales properly and the "closes" will look after themselves! You will have a much easier presentation, because you will be in complete control. Salespeople who try to sell without being in control have to rely on an awful lot of luck. Don't count on luck. It's like the showroom cat. It moves faster than you do.

13

EVERY ONE A WINNER

Have you ever heard the saying: "You can't win them all"? I thought so, it has become the salesperson's dictum.

Imagine yourself in the cockpit of a transatlantic Jumbo Jet, 450 passengers and crew, the pilot walks in, sits in his seat, turns on the ignition and rolls her down the runway. Just as she reaches take-off speed his co-pilot asks him a question: "Did you check the gas, captain?"

At several hundred mph and a couple of centimetres off the ground you would want to be fairly sure that the plane had a drop or two of fuel on board. And of course they are sure, they check first, in fact they have a check list.

A printed sheet which the co-pilot reads and the captain checks off before they even roll the beast out of its garage, let alone allow the wheels to start turning. These Jumbo jockeys are professional people. It's nice to know this when you are winging over an icy ocean in something that's too heavy to fly on its own and has all the buoyancy properties of a synchronised swimmer in concrete overboots.

And it doesn't end there. Once you're up, you have to come down. Being such an assured and accomplished flyer myself I try to extend the experience with half-a-dozen or so whiskys and chasers, taken for purely medicinal purposes, immediately prior to take-off. Anyway there you are hovering over a straight strip of concrete, and the tyres make that strange little squeal as they come into contact.

So now we're on the tarmac rolling along at speeds that would make Nigel Mansell envious, and we need to stop. But our captain's a heavy footed type and when he slams his size 12s onto the brake pedal, he snaps the cable. Not good, you may think.

Half a mile further on and we could be sitting in a very short Jumbo searching through the wreckage for our belongings, but

... searching through the wreckage for our belongings.

luckily, they've covered this problem, too. They're professionals. They have built in a back-up system; Boeing put in more than one brake cable.

Unlike we salesmen, the flyers believe that you *can* win them all, and it's a belief I desperately want to share, whenever I'm up there with them.

Every sales course I've ever been to, and every salesperson I've ever spoken to, accept the fact that you *can't* win them all. But I'm suggesting that a truly professional salesman, like a ruly professional airline pilot, has to win them all, and the methods they use to achieve this end, are remarkably similar.

The check list

All you need is a check list, and a back-up system, full of opportunities to win; the longer the list the better you will do.

In fact the only reason we lose, on most sales presentations, is because we went out there unprepared, we didn't provide ourselves with enough opportunities to win. That's where the check list comes in. If you sit down and write a list of sales objectives, in order of priority, it will not only give you opportunity to win every time, it'll also help you to remember what you are doing out there in the first place.

Our check list of objectives may look something like this:

* Sell the goods.
* Make a second appointment.
* Gather more information.
* Get a referral.
* Make a friend.

Sell the goods

There it is, written on a little card that you keep in your top pocket, "sell the product." On many occasions, I can remember watching a good prospect walking out of my showroom door, going home to "think about it." I'm standing staring at the back of his head, and running through my mind is the conversation we've just had.

We had a great time, we found out that we shared a common interest – motorcycling – we chatted away merrily about the T.T., who was the best rider, Surtees or Hailwood, Agostini or Sheene, Lawson or Mamola. We had a fine conversation about all the old British classic bikes, the ultimate technology of the latest Jap superbikes and the true quality of the BMWs and the Harley Davisons. Only one thing I missed, I didn't ask prospect if he wanted to buy.

And I know I'm not alone in this, it has become well established, by those academics who study such things, that over 60% of all sales presentations, trade or retail, end without the salesman having asked for the order.

Not me though, not nowadays, with my check list hot in my top pocket, before customer and I part company, I glance down at the list to see if I've covered everything, just like the pilot does, and if I haven't crossed this one off, then now's the time. If I haven't explicitly asked him if he wants to buy my goods, then I had better get asking!

The back-up system

Now comes the back-up system, if you have asked prospect if he wants to swap his money for your goods and he's said: "No." Then instead of going to sit in the office for half an hour, sucking your thumb until it goes all white and wrinkled, you must move on to step two.

Make a second appointment, if you can't persuade him to part with his hard-earned money this time, have a "reason to see him again," ready. A great number of sales are clinched at the second time of trying.

Back-up is most effective if you have a few options prepared before customer even steps through the door, those options could be things like:

"Fine, I can see why this model doesn't fit your bill. I tell you what, I have just what you're looking for coming in next week. I'll bring it around for you next Thursday evening. Tell me where you live."

or

"Yes I can see the benefit to you of financing the transaction with a bank loan, let's set a definite appointment for next Saturday, at this time. That'll give you the chance to sort the money out, and I can be sure to be here to see you."

or

"O.K. if you need time to think about it, why not take the weekend to think it over and I'll pop round to your office on Monday afternoon? I'll bring the goods and give you a full demonstration so that you can see how it performs in the working environment. That should help, shouldn't it?"

Like the boy scout, be prepared. Be prepared for the next prospect who walks in and wants to leave you without leaving his money.

Gather more information. Just suppose prospect has left without buying, neither would he allow you to set a second appointment. What can we do to "win" now? We could shuffle home, muttering dark oaths about all our customers, march into the house and give the budgie a good thump. But that won't help our bank balance.

Better is to dig for more information from the customer, about his needs and problems, and try to find ways to help him solve those problems in the future.

When you dig for further information, you find out that customer was planning to buy our product with money gained by cashing in some shares, but the market is depressed at the moment, and he would lose money by selling his shares now.

We dig for more information and find out what those shares are. Then we keep our eye on the stock market and contact him again when his shares have increased in value. We can become a delayed action winner, but a winner none the less.

You may simply ask for personal information about the buyer, his hobbies, his family, his career aspirations, his birthday, how many children he has, whether or not he enjoys the theatre, attending football or cricket matches, a night at the cinema. Is he a wine drinker, a car freak or whatever? Information which you can use, in all sorts of small ways, to win him over to buy from you.

For instance, if he's a snooker fan, you could send him tickets for the championship finals. If he's always admired Jaguar cars, you could send him the motoring magazine which is previewing the latest model. Anything no matter how small, to keep him thinking of you. If you do follow this plan, then you can be sure that he will buy from you eventually, the only way you can fail is if you don't try in the first place, or if you give up trying before he becomes a convert!

It is a more professional method than that employed by the cheeky salesman, who made his living selling encyclopaedias. When he got a "No" from his customers, he would pack up his samples, in complete silence, and walk to the door. As he reached the doorway he would stop and turn, and wearing his most hangdog expression he would ask his client for information, by saying:

"I'm very new to this selling game. I know we have the very best encyclopaedias on the market, and I know that our prices are lower than anyone else's. I can only think of one reason why you are not buying, it must be because of me. What did I do wrong?"

If customer felt sorry for him and tried to tell him, he was back in the sale!

Get a referral. Unless he's a really miserable dog, our prospect, by now, will be feeling a twinge or two of guilt. You have asked him for the sale – and he's said no. You have asked him if you can set a second appointment – and he's said no. You then went on to show great interest in him and his future needs – and he thinks that was nice of you.

So now when you ask if he knows anyone else, amongst his acquaintances, either at work or in his neighbourhood, who is looking to buy your goods, he'll be delighted to tell you. He won't mind ratting on his mates, it takes the pressure off him. And, unless he has a social problem, you end up with an alternative prospect, perhaps two, to work on.

Make a friend. When all else fails, and it rarely does, keep smiling, keep showing a genuine interest in Mr. Purchaser. It's the best way to make a friend of him, to motivate him through your door the next time he wants something that you may sell. If you make a friend, he'll be back.

There's our check list and back-up system, it's a comprehensive list that should keep us flying high. It gives us plenty of opportunities to win and we are bound to take at least one of them. It means that we will never again "crash-out" on a sale. We will win every time. Some days we'll win better than others, but we'll never again say: "You can't win them all!"

14

FEED YOURSELF WITH FEEDBACK

I've always been fascinated by the old 80/20 rule. When I first heard of it I was heavily into renovating old vehicles, well, let's be honest, I'd just bought this old wreck of a motorbike off an old mate. (I say old because when I took it home my dad said: "If ever I get 'old of 'im . . . !") Anyway, I was faced with the prospect of making this device roadworthy and I began to pick up a few engineering terms. Like oil. And I thought 80/20 was a multigrade. But it isn't.

Apparently, some brave scientists had been going around the world counting things, and when they fed their findings into a computer it came up with the amazing fact that just about everything that happens in this world adheres to the 80/20 rule. They prove this phenomenon with graphs and charts and areas under a curve and stuff that I'll never understand even after I've grown up.

They say that 80% of the sales are achieved by 20% of the salespeople for instance. 80% of the world's wealth is in the hands of 20% of the population. 80% of horse races are won by 20% of the runners. Guess who bets on the other four?

Scientists, being clever people, are the type that we should listen to, so I spoke to one. I haven't a clue what he said so I'm going to suggest that you consider this instead. When you're running through your sales presentation, there's an 80/20 rule, and to some salespeople this will come as quite a surprise. You should be doing 80% of the *listening* and only 20% of the talking.

If you are going to do 80% of the listening, it will be useful to know what you are listening for. You are trying to glean the needs which are really important to your customers, rather than those which you may assume your customer will be crazy about. Which brings me on to feedback. People buy for their reasons not yours, so you must find out what those reasons are and, equally important, you must remember them. Which brings me on to paper.

I don't care how good a memory you've got, it won't be as strong as that supplied by a biro and a sheet of paper. If you are going to be looking to them for feedback you may as well take notes and gather the information which may be used against them in evidence.

In most buying-selling situations the customer expects to be talked at, that's generally the way it is done.

Customer listens. Fast talking, untrustworthy, lying through his teeth salesman – talks. It has always been that way and it always will be. In your customer's mind. To this end customers will tell you things like "I'm only looking, thank you." "We have only just started to look." "We're only browsing at present." "We haven't even looked at all the brochures yet." "We're just thinking about it."

All of which means: "Leave us alone, we want to make our minds up without being conned by you."

Faced with this you have three options. You can leave them to it – and kiss them goodbye. You can ignore what they say and launch into descriptions of what you believe they may be interested in. Back to the old canned pitch, the old demarcation lines, customer versus salesman. Or you can ask them for feedback. Feedback is absolutely essential if you want to sell for your customer's reasons not your own.

Selling without feedback has often been compared with the old wartime ack-ack guns. Pumping bullet after bullet towards enemy aircraft, who have prudently moved on before the tracers reach them. Very few aircraft were ever shot down by ack-ack guns.

The modern equivalent is the heat-seeking or guided missile which locks onto its prey and follows wherever it goes. Feedback is like that missile, it allows you to zoom onto your customer's needs. An awful lot of planes have been shot down by feedback.

It is very easy to get feedback, just tell your customers that you want it. "Tell me what you have in mind for your new patio set?" It doesn't hurt a bit to ask questions like this and it's a sight easier than trying to remember a structured sales pitch.

Use silence to encourage feedback. Words will always rush in to fill a silence. All you need to ensure is that they are not your words. Silence can be used creatively. If you sense that your customer isn't listening to what you are saying. If she's thinking about what she's going to say when it is her turn to talk. Just stop talking. Don't even bother finishing what you are sayi . . . . If you have stopped, it must be their turn to start, and they will.

There is no point carrying on talking if customer isn't listening, take the time to do a little creative listening of your own. He who talks may dominate the conversation, but he who asks the questions and then listens, will easily control it.

It always helps to watch what your customer is doing while you are talking to him; eye-to-eye contact is especially useful. People believe that those whose eyes are flicking everywhere except into their own are "shifty-eyed" and cannot be trusted. Innocents on the other hand are wide-eyed and trustworthy.

Open questions
The greatest gatherers of feedback that we can use are the questions which cannot easily be answered with the words "yes" or "no." Such questions begin with: "Who," "What," "Why," "Where," "How," and "When". Open questions which encourage our customers to explain exactly what they have in mind.

Open questions can be so useful when you are trying to win

round a reluctant customer who would really, rather not talk to you. At least not pleasantly. Here is a showroom that sells kitchen units.

Nigel and Nina Niggardly walk in one bright and sunny morning. Almost immediately, the sun goes in and it starts to rain.

Sweet innocent Stephanie Salesperson approaches with a smile: "Hello. How can I help you?"

"You can't luv. We're just looking!", grizzles Nigel, muttering to Nina at the same time about the stupidity of looking at new kitchens when they have the perfectly good one, which he built for her 25 years ago.

We've all had charmers like these two haven't we? We've all felt the temper rising in our throats that these cretins have the ability to make us feel as welcome as lepers, and on our own premises too. These types wouldn't give you the time of day, let alone any feedback. But Stephanie is made of sterner stuff, a few well aimed questions and she'll pass on to gathering the info.

Steph: "Fine, I won't pester you. But just take a look inside the units. There are all kinds of goodies hidden away behind the doors. Pull-out tables. Shelves which revolve right around, or pull out towards you, to make it easier to find things."

"Humph. Bloody gadgets!", interjects Nigel. "I didn't need gadgets in the kitchen I built, just good solid cupboards!"

Stephanie decides to take control: "It must be very difficult to build your own kitchen. Tell me, *how* did you do it?"

"Huh. Dead easy. I've always been good with me hands, haven't I Nina?"

"*What* kind of wood did you use?" Stephanie asks, smiling sweetly.

Nigel starts to tell her, she smiles again and he's away. He has found a person who is showing interest in him and his expertise. Someone who is asking him about the subject rather than stuffing him full of, what he sees as, nonsense.

"With the new materials about these days, if you were going

to remake your kitchen, *how* would you feel about making the units out of laminated boarding?" soothes Steph.

Nigel considers for a while and says: "Well I think the old plywood construction was better, but I don't have time these days, and they all seem to use chipboard, so perhaps I would use that."

"Yes, you are very wise. The modern boardings are so well manufactured that they make a perfect material for kitchen cabinets. *What* type of kitchen had you in mind? An oak door or a laminate?" And she's in, the sun is peeping out from behind the clouds and Nigel is listening to her.

Stephanie has asked questions to overcome his initial reluctance and to make friends. Now that friendship has to be turned into a sale. She just carries on gathering feedback until she knows what turns Nigel and Nina on.

Reward feedback

If you have a dog, you will know that if you pat him on the back and rub his tummy, he'll wag his tail and give you some

If that's what you want Nigel to do, follow the same methods.

affection. If that's what you want Nigel to do, follow the same methods. If it's feedback you're after though, some other form of reward is called for. You must always reward feedback even if it is unwelcome, that way you will get some more.

You: "What brought you in to see us?"

Them: "Well a friend of ours had one of your products. They weren't very impressed with you, but we thought we would come and see you anyway."

That's feedback and must be rewarded. "Thanks for telling me, I'm very glad you had the courage to come in. Tell me who your friend is and I will see if I can do anything to help put things right."

In situations like this, the first reaction is to argue with your customers. But if you do they won't feel inclined to give you any feedback, they won't be too ready to give you their money either. If you argue you can't win. You may win the point but you're sure to lose the sale.

If anyone expresses an opinion that you believe to be utter twaddle, a good phrase to help keep things on a level keel is: "Fine ... I can understand why you feel that way ... my own experience has been this ... how does that help?"

Nina Niggardly: "I think these fan cookers are rubbish. My friend has one and it is always breaking down."

Stephanie: "Yes, with an experience like that, I can see why you would feel that way. My own experience of fan cookers is that it very much depends on the make. Some brands are nothing but trouble, but I can show you some which are very reliable. How do you feel about that?"

There is no such thing as negative feedback. At the very least you find out what your prospect is thinking. If that offends, you can react accordingly. You remain in control.

Nigel: "You've got a big nose. I don't like saleswomen with big noses. I don't like you!"

Stephanie: "Fine, you must have had a bad experience with a big nosed saleswoman. I can understand that you would feel that way. My own experience is that big noses are purely hereditary, usually handed down from father to daughter. Did you ever have a father?"

Probe and listen
In the first chapter, I described what happened when my wife went to buy a new car. How do you think Fred was able to re-open the sale to my wife, after Dennis, his colleague had done his best to drive her away?

Fred used a different tack from Dennis; instead of plugging away with a practised sales pitch he asked questions, and listened. It went like this: "Hello Mrs. Moss are you leaving?"

"Yes!!!"

"What had you come in for?"

"I wanted to look at the Charleston but..."

"Oh, here you are. I've got the keys in my pocket. Take it for a spin round the block."

He smiled broadly: "It's a beautiful little car. What made you choose that one?"

"Well it's a bit silly really... it's just... well... I love the colour."

"Me too," grinned Fred, "it really does look classy doesn't it?"

Then the rat lowered his voice, bent slightly towards her and said: "And do you know what? They've just brought out a new body protection process; this car is one of the first to have it. It means that your Charleston will look as good in five years, as it does this morning."

With that he handed her the keys and I could feel the numbers flowing from my bank account.

Like Fred, you will be far better paid for asking the correct questions, than for thinking that you know all the answers. And if your first aim is to get your customers giving you feedback, it will almost certainly encourage them to end up by giving you an order.

15

EARS THE ANSWER

It had been so long since I bought my last motor-bike that it was British. A B.S.A. Bantam.

But with life just about to begin again, all sorts of odd feelings and desires were surfacing. One of them being to buy myself the biggest, meanest, fastest bike in the world.

It was to be my present to me for the special birthday and it had to be so fast that I would get back to 21 again.

I'm prepared to accept that not many business-suited 40-year-olds walk in to buy motor-cycles but this was a very large dealership and they must have had some mature clientele, so when the young salesman said to me: "Hmmm the fastest motor-cycle. Is it for your son? How old is he? Does he have a full licence?"

I said: "Yes." Took his leaflet on the JetBlaster 1200 and left.

Three days later and I tried again. I went in by a side door hoping to avoid the young salesman, walked up to the JetBlaster and sat astride.

Within seconds I was dreaming of the old days, I really did love that Bantam. I had taken it to bits and put it together again so many times I had pieces to spare. Everything that could be oiled, painted or polished, had been. It gleamed.

It did 35 mph flat out in second, and 40 mph in top! Geoff Duke, John Surtees, what did they know?

Salesman number two brought me crashing out of my day dream. "Oh, it's for you is it?"

Me: "Yes."

Him: "Well you don't want this bike. It'll be far too fast. Come and look at the SloshAlong 500, it is the most comfortable, reliable bike on the road today."

Me: "But .. but .. I want ..." Now I have a leaflet on the JetBlaster and a leaflet on the SloshAlong and I leave quietly.

I never was one to give in too easily and, sure enough, next day I was back again. I crept surreptitiously around the showroom, eyes peeled for the salesmen who didn't want to sell me the fastest, meanest, biggest bike on two wheels.

There it was glimmering in the full blow of five high powered spotlights. I wondered how close I'd get before one of them tapped me on the shoulder and said: "Can I help you?"

Me: "Tell me how fast the JetBlaster goes."

Him: "Ah the JetBlaster. It's got belt drive you know."

Me: "No I didn't know." Thinking: 'Belt drive doesn't sound very fast'.

Him: "And it's got an electric starter with auto decompression."

Me: "Oh, does that make it go faster?"

Him: "It has hydraulic valve adjusters and automatic cam chain tensioners, which means very low maintenance."

Me: "Do they help the top speed?"

Him: "Well, no but the oil cooled four cylinder, four valve, turbo charged engine does. But you won't be going faster than 70 mph, will you? By the way have you considered the Sloshalong?"

Me: "No! Tell me about the turbo charger. And the four valves per cylinder. And the four cylinder engine. What's the top speed?"

I was beginning to think that I was on to a winner but he hadn't heard me. He was still rattling on about braking efficiency, suspension balance, weather protection, the possibility of hanging luggage carriers, and all the rest of the boring stuff that turned this magnificent machine into the best cruiser on British roads. He didn't even notice when I crept out the door.

I didn't want a cruiser I wanted a full blown racer.

By this time I was familiar with the schedule of this showroom and right about now was the time when these sales stars went down to the pub for a sandwich. So I meandered around the second-hand car lot next door.

As soon as they took off for lunch I was back. I had been examining the bike for a good five minutes before this old chap emerged. He was the proprietor and he'd been hidden away in his back office, where he spends the day worrying about sales figures. He asked me what I wanted.

I almost daren't say it. "I think I'm interested in the JetBlaster 1200."

"Oh. Why do you think that?" This was strange. Apart from being much nearer my age, this chap wanted to know things about me.

So I said: "Well, it's just that . . ." (Pause) "Is the JetBlaster fast?"

"Is it fast?" His smile lit both sides of his face at once: "It goes like a politician's promise." This man knew where I was coming from. He'd already been there. He was my friend.

I cried: "Oh boy! How fast will it go?"

"We can't really say. The makers are encouraged not to put top speed on the leaflets these days," he quipped handing me another brochure.

"It says in here that the JetBlaster lapped the Isle of Man at more than 120 mph, and it's got 160 mph on the speedo. Will it do that?" I pleaded.

"It's not that I want to be awkward," he said, "It's just that the authorities take a very dim view of motor-cycle dealers and manufacturers who romanticise the danger element to youngsters who are easily influenced."

"I'm not young," I whimpered, "look I've got grey hair." He stooped to wipe my dribble off his shoes as I stood open-mouthed listening to my new friend. "Aw go on, tell me what she'll do."

He shook my arms loose from his left ankle and said: "Well I shouldn't really. I'm a respectable businessman now." He pondered for a second or two before continuing: "I was cruising just outside Lincoln. On the old Roman Ramper. Straight as a die for mile after mile and the moon was shining full to blind you. I could see so far my goggles cracked, and not another vehicle in sight. So I thought, this is it. Give her a twist." His eyes had glazed over.

I prompted, "Yeah!"

He said. "She leapt forward so fast I had to hook my toes under the handlebars to stay with her. The wind was howling

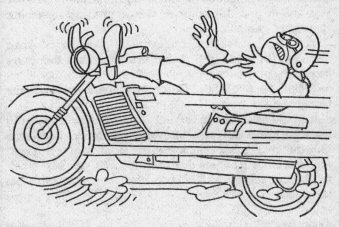

"She leapt forward so fast I had to hook my toes under the handlebars to stay with her."

round my crash hat and a million moths were swooping, as the snow, into my face. I was 18 again. God it felt good."

I had both arms around his shoulders, staring intently into his eyes. "How fast will she go?"

"I don't rightly know."

"What do you mean you don't know." I croaked.

"I ran out of bottle before the needle had gone full circle, but just before I did that the speedo was showing 144 mph." His eyes drifted back into focus.

I could hardly say it: "One - hundred - and - forty - four - mph."

He said. "Do you think you'll pay cash, or shall I get the finance forms sorted?"

I just handed him my cheque book and said: "Have your way with me."

Defeat the enemies
One of the biggest enemies of any salesman is talking about features and benefits that are of absolutely no interest to the customer. Plugging away blindly with all the information at your fingertips and just hoping that you will say something that lights your customer up.

This chap just asked me one question: "Why do you think you want the Jetblaster?" And then all we talked about was speed. The only thing I was interested in. He was using all his sales skills to sell only that feature that this customer was hot for.

It would have been so easy for him to let flow with all the knowledge that his experience with motorcycles had given him, but this salesman had a keen appreciation of two things; first, it is far better to ask than to tell. Second, your ears are so much more effective as selling devices than your mouth is, so use them.

Take it away again
He had also learnt how to build up desire, by taking away the support that he had shown himself capable of giving. This technique is particularly useful when you are dealing with a customer who is saying that they want your product, but only if the terms of the sale are unreasonably angled to suit their every need.

The "take it away from them" technique was best

illustrated to me early on in my career after I had come close to losing patience with a very important prospect. He was a distributor, selling to trade outlets nationwide. We were a small company, selling through our own retail outlet and to some local trade outlets. His initial approach was about the most exciting thing that had happened to us so far.

It also happened that our product was a perfect complement to the range that he sold. At our initial contact he was making all the running, perhaps we could do business, IF the price was right, IF we could give him exclusivity on certain items, IF we could assure him priority of delivery, IF, IF, IF. It began to look as though all our future production would have to be geared to his needs.

My religion on that matter is: that if you have all your eggs in one basket, that basket must be perfect, and it's a silly basket that believes it is. I was feeling less than thrilled, so I stopped selling, and started to take away all the things he was asking for.

"It will be a great pity, but I don't think we're going to be able to give you those delivery times. You see we are a developing company and until we make the move to our new premises, then I rather fear that we won't be able to supply you fast enough. Perhaps we will be better off looking for someone with more modest needs."

As soon as I'd uttered these words a remarkable thing happened. He began to backpedal; he really was interested in buying our goods and the thought of losing us as a source of supply made him even keener to do business.

I wasn't being clever, I'd just lost patience with him. I stumbled over the technique purely by accident, but have since found it to work with any customer who is making unreasonable demands, or voicing an unreasonable complaint against your company.

Customer: "I'm so fed up with the time it takes your service men to reach us, when the equipment breaks down, that I'm seriously considering taking on another supplier."

You: "Fine, I can understand that speed of service is of prime importance to you, however we do give a guaranteed call-out time of 16 working hours, which is eight hours better than our nearest rival. We will not be able to improve on that time, so perhaps the most civilised thing we can do is to thank each other for all the successful business that we have done in the past and part company amicably. We do need a committed dealer in this area!" You'll soon find out how serious the problem is and you'll find yourself holding the reins, rather than being driven scatty by an unreasonable demand.

The key word of course is "unreasonable". If the customer has a justified complaint your answer is slightly different. You say: "Sorry."

I'm off to have a little fun now. Just lately I've been going out about this time. Waiting until those boy-salesmen pour out of the dealership on their Yamuki LRX650's. When they do I'm going to shower them with mud and exhaust fumes from the back of the biggest, meanest, fastest bike in the world. Roll on retirement age!

16

ASKING FOR THE SALE

There's an old saying in selling, and it is so obvious most of us forget it. It's like a pine cone in a plantation, unless the cone lets go of its branch and stabs you in the eyeball, you never see it.

The saying is: "Always ask for the sale!"

Just as the pine trees couldn't have grown without that cone, their seed; so your sales won't grow unless you ask.

Having decided to earn my living in the heady atmosphere of salesmanship, and being one who does not believe in work for work's sake, it soon became very important to me to hone and expand my sales skills to make the job of earning my living as simple as possible.

I have not only spent time studying the subject, I have actually spent money on it too. I still earn the greatest part of my living standing face to face with customers, however, I have found that speaking and writing about the subject is a great spur to the concentration.

If, in the course of a presentation, you tell your customer something which, unbeknown to you, is inaccurate, there is a strong chance that you will escape with your reputation unblemished. They are probably not listening properly and you are only aiming that inaccuracy at one or two individuals who most likely know no better than you, or if they do, are swayed to your way of thinking by the force of your

personality. Write that inaccuracy down in black and white
and the rules change; your statements are open to detailed
examination by anyone. Accuracy becomes paramount.

When I first heard it suggested that almost three quarters
of salespeople conclude their presentations without having
directly asked for the order, I was highly sceptical. So I began
to take notice, firstly of what I did, then of what those who
came to sell to me did, as well as to what those who worked
for me did. My scepticism was slowly eroded. I came to the
stunning conclusion that no matter what was being sold, nor
to whom; almost seven out of ten sales presentations end
without the salesperson having asked for the order.

Salesperson has accurately determined what the customer
needs to buy, has demonstrated the features of his product
that match those needs, so now it is time to move towards the
closing sequence. After all if a job is worth doing, it is worth
doing for money.

But something like 70% of salespeople don't ask for the
money! Isn't that stupid, a salesman not asking for a sale?

Picture a showjumper, doesn't he look magnificent
prancing into the ring, little puffs of sawdust kicking up
under the beast's hooves. The rider, clad in scarlet, aims his
horse at the first fence. He slows his horse to balance its step
and then launches it at the poles. Horse surges gamely
forward but, receiving no command from rider, ploughs
straight on through, leaving behind it a mess of planks and
conifers, and a puce coloured course-builder.

He's the 25th horse to enter the ring that day, but so far let's
suppose only eight have attempted to jump that first fence.
Now, I can't say that showjumping is my favourite sport, but
some people find it stimulating and exciting to watch. Can
you imagine though, how boring we would all find the
commentator's words if, out of 100 riders, only thirty
attempted to jump the fences?

The riders can't hope to get a clear round if they don't
attempt to jump the fences; salesmen cannot hope to close

many sales if they don't ask their customers to buy.

Learning not to ask

I've been developing another theory lately, concerning company representatives. The salespeople who come into my retail shop, and try to sell me their goods, seem to have lost all the old natural skills. I put it down to too much coaching.

These reps are sent on intensive sales training courses which teach them all the current trends on persuading retailers to buy their brand of goods. They come out of that seven day course as sophisticated salesmen. People who already know that it's no good just asking for the sale, that selling is a lot harder than that.

Perhaps if these fresh-faced rookies were left to their own devices they would be so inexperienced that they would come in and ask me if I would like to order some of their produce. Probably I would be so taken aback by their openness that I would whip out my ball-point and sign them an order.

Such a thing could never happen with old hands. They know all the objections I might have, they have heard them all before. They are certain that to sell anything to Mr. Retailer takes sophisticated sales techniques. They are worldly and experienced. They know for definite that we wizened old shopkeepers expect them to do battle, and until blood is spilt, no orders will be signed. Just to say: "Do you want to buy?" won't do.

And that's where the greatest mistake, made by salespeople today, originates. Seventy per cent don't say "do you want to buy?" They don't bother to jump the fences!

They've done all the rest. They've bought the horse, and the hunting jacket, and the hat. They've trained over every jump imaginable, they've bought a horse box and a Range-Rover to tow it to the event, they've warmed-up, entered the ring, and then they plough straight through the first jump acquiring more faults than I've got!

... they plough straight through the first jump acquiring more faults
than I've got!

Learning how often to ask
And it's worse than that, Jim. Upon hearing the responses:
"No thanks" – "not today" – "I'd like to think it over" –
"Clear off and stop pestering me." All different forms of Nos.
Of those 30% who do ask for the order:-

    10 give up after one refusal.
    Another 7 give up after two refusals.
    Another 3 give up after three refusals.
    Another 2 give up after four refusals.

All of this means that, after four fences, only eight of the
original 100 riders are still in the saddle, the rest are in the car
park, trying to prise fence posts out of Dobbin's nostrils.
Think about the odds!

It eventually dawned on me that a great many buyers said:
"No thanks," several times, before they said, "Yes please."
My own calculations on this indicated that some 60% of

buyers said: "NO!" four times before they finally said yes. This is my theory; you may check it out and find the figures are slightly different for you, but I'd bet they're not a lot different. So, what I'm saying is that the eight salespeople still asking for the order after four refusals are likely to pick up at least 60% of the business, and they will do it just by asking.

Here it is, we have discovered the key to successful selling: you ask, you get. And the more times you ask, the more you get. Why then do so many salespeople consistently fail to ask for business?

Perhaps it's because salesman himself has been on the receiving end of "high-pressure salesmanship" and agrees with all those of his customers who say that they will never buy from high pressure salesmen. The fact is though that a great majority of people do buy from these methods, not perhaps the most professional, but mighty effective nonetheless.

If you look down your nose at high pressure techniques (and you need a distinct lack of sensitivity not to scorn them), then rest assured that you are not being "high pressure," simply because you ask; asking is just doing a professional job.

Learning when to ask

Perhaps it is because salesman isn't really sure when to ask.

Remember that sales seminar I went to, the one which majored on closing the sale? Well, they said: "There is only one way to learn when to ask for the sale, that is by closing early, closing often and closing hard." Being one of a trusting nature, I tried it. I closed early, my customers walked out; I closed often, they acted like I wasn't there; I closed hard, they questioned me on the existence of my father.

Eventually I concluded that it was easier not to close at all; why should I when it hurt?

"Hang on," you may well cry. "First you tell us to ask, now you are saying that, if we do, we are asking for trouble." Of course that's not what I'm saying, but I am saying that it helps if you get the timing right.

In every successful sale there is a "purple patch," when our customer is ready to sign the order. Experienced salespeople will be able to pick up the "buying signals" and know instinctively when to close the sale. But until that sixth sense is developed we need some guidance to tell us when the time is right.

If we close too soon, we will get an objection or be put off. If we close too late, we will most probably talk ourselves out of the sale. Far more sales are lost by the salesmen missing the purple patch, and talking through it, than by closing too soon.

17

TIMING THE CLOSE

Right. Now you understand the need to ask for the sale every time you present your wares, and the need to detect the "purple patch" in that sale, when customer is most likely to shower you in signed cheques. But how do you spot it?

It should encourage you to know that if I can do a thing it has to be simple. If it were hard I would still be in bed pretending to be poorly!

This bit is easy. Learn that, at any one time, your customers can hold only one of three attitudes. They will either "object" to what you are saying; be "indifferent" to what you are saying; or will "accept," your every word.

Three alternatives: Objection, Indifference or Acceptance. You can determine whether or not your customer is ready to part with their money, by a simple process of elimination.

Let's have a look at these three attitudes, see how best to recognise them and work out how best to deal with them.

Easy objections

Objections are part of every sales process and are amongst the strongest buying signals you will be sent. Things like: "You are too expensive, I only wanted to spend half that." "I don't like the colour, it won't match my new curtains." "The delivery is too slow, I wanted the whole thing completed before then." Objections like these, tell you that customer is interested in your goods. Not interested enough to buy yet, but you have what they want.

Training courses devote a great deal of time to overcoming objections. Some say that the sale begins only when an objection comes up. Until that has happened, we are simply taking orders. All red-blooded salesmen should see an objection as an invitation to lock horns with the foe, to use all his training and skills to outwit his opponent in a battle of wills. After all where's the fun, they say, if they give in too easily.

What a load of codswallop. An objection means that your customer thinks he has a problem and he is letting you know what that problem is.

More often than not, the main objection is price. There won't be many salespeople around who haven't experienced this:

You sell room lighting. Daphne Warner-Byone has come down to London for the day, she is looking for a crystal chandelier for the hallway in her farmhouse: "Yes young man it's just what I want but it's dweadfully expensive."

Average salesman – worrying that this objection is going to lose him the sale – attacks the statement with: "Oh no, you're wrong there. Chandeliers of this quality are worth every penny of the price we are asking. In fact, this particular luminaire is on special offer this week, so the price we are showing is very competitive."

Daphne doesn't like being wrong, she begins to defend her position, to prove that she's right and that the chandelier is extremely expensive. The more she says about the light costing so much, the more she believes it and pretty soon, the objection is growing into a real problem.

A top-class salesperson, would probably answer the question with: "Yes these chandeliers do cost a lot of money, don't they?"

He is withholding support, either negative or positive. Leaving the farmer's wife out there all alone with a non-threatening, neutral statement. He shows her that he understands her viewpoint, but does not argue with it.

He could just as easily have said: "I understand." – "Uh huh," or remained silent.

It is a good rule to ignore the first objection, to test out whether it is a real objection, or simply something customer is saying just for the sake of saying something. You will find that the majority of objections, when ignored, will go away never to be heard from again.

Not many salespeople are comfortable with this technique, they want to get stuck in and start persuading. But trust me. If the objection is really important to the customer, it will raise its ugly head again.

Us: "I understand."

Warner-Byone: "What on earth do you mean, you understand? This light is ridiculously expensive."

Good, now we have an objection that is important to our customer and the time has come to deal with it.

Unless you get a violent reaction first time, ignore the objection. Only when it comes up a second time, is an objection worthy to merit our concern.

So let's look at one step-by-step method for handling objections. We'll stick with price, because, unless you are giving stuff away, you will meet it on a regular basis.

Customer says: "I'm sorry but you are just too expensive."

You spent time, when you opened the sale, developing rapport with this customer, you are their friend, you will go along with them and minimise any resistance.

You show your ability to deal with the objection with a statement such as: "Good, that's an interesting point you've brought up and I'm delighted that you have. Now we can discuss it."

You are back to rewarding feedback, even this type which you are not too thrilled to hear. At least you will get to know what the objection is and get the opportunity to try and deal with it.

The next step is to confirm that you have understood what the objection is. It does no good overcoming objections if you are working on the wrong objection in the first place. Because you haven't understood what the customer meant.

To do that, you re-state the objection until you describe the customer's worries to his complete satisfaction. If he says: "No, that's not what I mean." You have to keep rephrasing, asking back. You cannot proceed with the objection until you are in complete agreement what that objection is.

Daphne Warner-Byone again: "It's just too expensive, Randolph would be furious if I spent that much."

You: "Are you saying that it is more than you can afford to pay?"

Daphne: "No, of course not, we could afford ten of them, it is just more than I want to pay."

You: "Do you mean then that you have seen a chandelier somewhere else, that was just what you wanted, but cost much less?"

Daphne: "Well our local electrical shop has something similar but at a much lower price."

Now you have it. The amount of money isn't the objection. Husband Randolph isn't going to stop her. You have some competition that's all. You can handle competition, you're used to it.

Before you do though, move on to step three, you must isolate the objection.

You: "Just to clarify things in my mind Mrs. Warner-Byone, price apart, is there anything else that prevents us from going ahead now?"

It is no good spending your energy and time overcoming an objection if she's going to hit you with another one as soon as your back's turned. You want her money, not a game of customer object, salesman overcome it.

There's another danger of course, and that is that dear old Daph may be thinking up objections as a polite way of telling you to go away. If that is the case, then don't waste your time, flow with her and get out of the way.

Simply and politely say: "Do you really want a chandelier,

or are you wondering how to get rid of me? If you are, just say so and I'll go. If you want a chandelier however, I'm happy to stay and work that one out with you." Smile broadly while you are saying it but don't be afraid to be so blunt, it will often bring out the true problem. At worst they will know not to mess you about.

Daphne isn't trying to get rid and says: "Oh no, I would like the chandelier, it's just your price that is over the top."

You are on to step four, you have a real objection and you have to deal with it. Before you do, quantify it, using her own words ask: "How much over the top is it?"

Price is usually a pretty easy objection and as such should be dealt with head on. Price will only be a difficult objection when your customer doesn't want to buy badly enough. You have a good idea that your farmer's wife wants your chandelier, because she is still talking to you.

Your chandelier is a real beauty, her answer is: "Well if it were £200 less then I would be interested."

Perhaps you are able to discount the item by £200 and still remain profitable. If so, you have her money. But that's too easy.

Perhaps there is a delivery charge built in to the price; if so you could suggest that she take the chandelier with her. In that case you may get a little closer. But let's say that it is not the case; you can do nothing to lower the price.

You only have two alternatives, sell her a different chandelier that costs £200 less, always assuming she likes it better than the one which your competitor is offering. More likely though, is that you will find yourself trying to reduce the difference, £200, to something more realistic.

This is fairly easy to do if you take into account how long the fitting is likely to be hung in that old farmhouse.

You: "As I understand it, we have £200 difference between what you would be happy paying for this chandelier and the other one you have seen."

Warner-Byone: "That's right."

You: "Would you write this down please?"

Hand her your best pen and a clean sheet of paper; if she does the mathematics, she will believe it, they will be her numbers. Also she won't write down anything she doesn't understand, she cannot feel that you are trying to trick her.

You: "A magnificent chandelier of this quality will last a lifetime, but let's suppose that in ten years' time, you will tire of seeing it and pass it on to one of the children, for their homes. Does that seem fair?"

Daphne: "Well I suppose so, but I expect it to be there much longer than ten years."

You: "Divide our £200 by ten years."

Her: "Yes £20." She's wondering exactly what you are up to.

You: "Now divide that £20 by twelve months."

She's getting in to this now: "Yes that's £1.67." If she wants to borrow a calculator, hand her one, let her do the button-pressing.

You: "Smashing, £1.67 per month, now divide that by four to get the weekly amount."

Her: "Yes that's about 42 pence."

Us: "So to have the chandelier which you really want, rather than the one that you feel you have to settle for, is going to cost a mere 42 pence per week extra. That's 6p per day, 3p in the morning and 3p in the afternoon. Imagine what 3p will be worth in 10 years' time! Are you really going to settle for second-best on such a small sum?"

You have done your utmost, you have reduced the price to the ridiculous, but more than that, you have painted a picture in her mind of just how unimportant the price is, if she really wants your product.

Difficult objections

Not all objections are as easy to handle as price, difficult objections need a different technique. Difficult, by the way, means those objections for which you have no good answers.

You will know all the examples of difficult objections to the products you sell, without my bringing them out of the closet.

The best way to deal with difficult objections is to introduce additional benefits, which are of interest to the customer.

If you didn't cover every conceivable benefit during the sales presentation then now is the time. Try to prove benefits of ownership which will minimise their objection.

One or two objections though are common to all sales-people. Say you have a customer who doesn't truly trust that your product is capable of doing what you claim it will do. How do you get round that one? Here's where a file of written testimonials earns its corn.

In a situation where you are selling to doubting Thomas, if you could say: "I understand your worry that perhaps we are not quite as good as we say. However if I had one or a number of past clients in this room with us, right now, would you be guided by what they say?"

Customer must answer: "Yes."

Which leaves you to reply: "Well obviously they are not here. However, this is what they have written about us."

There is no hard and fast route through difficult objections but evidence, in the form of letters and photographs, from a testimonial file, can be a very powerful aid to overcoming difficult objections.

This is probably the only time, within your sale, when you should not be afraid to furnish customer with graphs, statistics and statements from bodies of authority, to back up what you are saying.

Let's suppose someone says your price for fitting the carpets in their new home is too high, that Bert Bodgit can do the job for much less. You may be able to refer to the detail in both quotes and point out that Bert has left so many things (that you have included) off his quote and that he is actually more expensive, for what he is doing.

Maybe customer has a friend, who knows an electrician,

and customer's friend says that the lighting you have recommended is not up to the safety standard. You can show the full specification, including the British Standard number for the lights in question, and take away his fears.

Customer shows concern that the solar heating panels that he is thinking of installing, to provide him with free hot water, may get so hot on sunny summer days, that the reflected heat will burn the feathers off his prize pigeons as they pass over the roof, at the end of a long race. You furnish details from the pigeon fanciers association which endorse the use of such panels and prove their beneficial effect on the breeding cycle of prize birds.

Normally we are well advised to shy away from technical data during a sale, but at times like this they can be very useful.

The very best way to handle objections, both difficult and easy, is by doing such a thorough job of determining your customer's every whim and demonstrating how your products will effectively match those whims that you eliminate all objections before you get to this stage. But this life doesn't always span out like that!

Indifference
Don't you just know when customer is indifferent to your sales presentation? You can tell by the yawns and the fact that they keep wandering off, leaving you to chat away to the backs of their heads.

They say things like: "Well, thank you for your time but we're not in a hurry to do the work yet," or "The one we have is O.K. We only came in to get out of the rain .. to pick your brains .. to see if you had anything new," or "George is a keen DIYer; we're just looking for ideas."

From the point of view of selling them something, you won't – not yet. They are not sold on you or your products, they are not convinced that what you have to offer will make their present situation more comfortable.

Indifference stems from four basic negatives. Either they don't fully trust you. – They are not aware of a need for your products and services. – They do need your products but are not sold on the idea that you can help to satisfy their needs. – They are in no hurry, they know that you have what they want but they don't want it yet.

If you can recognise and deal with these four negatives; no trust; no need; no assistance and no hurry, then you will turn that indifference into a sale.

To deal with indifference you ask a particular type of question. Suggestive questions! Questions which start customer thinking about areas where he may be dissatisfied with his present situation. Very often, simply by your motivating customer to talk about his situation he will discover what problems he has and what solution he needs to apply, with no persuasion from you needed.

We have shown that the best probing questions start with the words How, What, Where, Why, When and Who. That is certainly the case when you want to gather information. But in this case you don't really need answers. This time, your questions are simply a vehicle designed to implant into your customer's mind the awareness that he has a problem, and in particular, that he has a problem which you can solve.

Such questions will draw his attention to areas you think should be addressed, areas he has probably overlooked.

Staying with room lighting, the questions could be: "Are you aware of the present regulations for rewiring the lighting in your home?"

Or: "If I could save you ££s a year on your lighting bill, would you still rather have the work done next year?"

Or: "Do you know how much greater the fire risk is for unqualified people doing their own home electrical work?"

Or: "What kind of insurance cover have you got, does it cover damage which you may cause yourself?"

One classic example of this was the electrician that my friend called in to see to a fuse which kept failing.

Friend said: "Ever since I put those extra fluorescents in the garage, the fuse has been blowing and when we switch the house lights on, they go dim now and again."

Electrician was in to mend a fuse, he said: "Let's see what you've done." Took one look and sighed: "Where did you put the superdooper auto-reset consumer unit breaker box (or some such technical wording), that you need to avoid the risk of fire with so many lights?" He sold a week's work, plus expensive electrical hardware, just by implanting into my friend's mind an awareness of the need to have the lethal electrical work, that he had done himself, put right by a professional. An awareness which had not been there before.

He didn't need a reply to his question, my friend's guilty silence spoke volumes.

Acceptance

The instant Daphne Warner-Byone utters the magic words: "Yes, I'm sure Randolph wouldn't begrudge me 6p a day", you close.

As soon as your customer shows signs of acceptance you stop making conversation and go for it. To carry on selling the goods at this point will most likely carry you through the purple patch, and out of a sale.

Lots and lots of salespeople do just that. They could have had a sale after two minutes, but two hours of introducing and overcoming objections leaves them with a well educated and slightly bemused prospect who slopes out of the shop to think about all that has been said.

So you have got the green light and you are going to grab for it. How?

The first closing technique I ever used was succinct and to the point, in fact it only consisted of one word: "Well?" People found it impossible not to reply to this dazzling skill and usually answered: "Yes I'm fine thanks. Goodbye."

So I really started motoring, I developed: "O.K. people, what do you think?" They told me.

Then I hit on a new idea, I would look them forlornly in the eye and say: "How about it?"

If they still weren't sure what "it" was, if they didn't force their money on me – I'd go for the big one – I'd grab them round the right ankle, and as they dragged me screaming towards the exit, would plead: "Think about my kids, if you don't buy, how will I earn the money to feed them?"

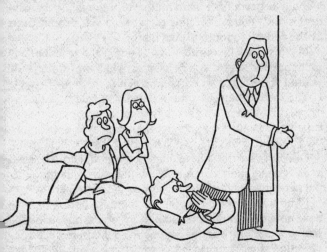

"Think about my kids, if you don't buy, how will I earn the money to feed them?"

Aren't people hard? Even with such subtle and effective methods I was finding the close difficult. My boss suggested a career in the dairy products industry, delivering milk, but I just knew he was joking.

I thought I did quite well as a milkman but the old pull of selling was too strong to deny and before long I was back at it. I went to a seminar, remember, 55 unique and original closes they taught me.

"Do you want to sign with the red pen, or the blue?" Can't

recommend that one, not when the only writing implements within walking distance are one of the kid's broken crayons and the pencil, whose lead drops quietly onto the desk before your very eyes. You do feel daft having to ask to borrow two pens don't you?

"Would you like delivery by the 17th or would the 24th suit you best?" Good one, as long as customer doesn't say "You'd better have it here by the 10th, boyo, or the whole deal is off." You ain't feeling quite so suave and sophisticated at the end of a mouthful like that.

My personal favourite was: "Your place or mine?" But even that one got to be very painful. When she replied, "ohh yours I think"; my wife gave me hell.

The logic behind all these "alternative" closes is that you aren't asking them whether they want to buy or not, that step is being smoothed over to give them an easier decision. Not "Do I want to buy?" but "When do I want it delivered?"

Of course we don't need 55 closes, one will do. The close I have become most comfortable with is that of summarizing the benefits which are important to the customer.

I know what these benefits are, because during the sale I have noted down the most important points and, as soon as the customer's attitude has swung from indifference, through objection to acceptance, I say something along these lines.

"Fine Mrs. Warner-Byone, let me just be sure on the things which you have told me are important to you."

People buy for their reasons not ours.

"You wanted a top-quality crystal chandelier that will really suit your entrance hall, and this is the one. You want it delivered before your dinner party on Saturday the 15th, and we can have it there by the ninth. You want it installed and the workmen out of the way before your caterers move in, and we have organised that for the tenth, giving you almost a clear week to prepare for the party. All we need to get started is your signature and deposit. Sign here please."

Job done. But what if it isn't, what if I have misjudged her attitude? What if she wasn't ready to accept my product? What if I have missed the purple patch? I could be wrong, it has been known, but if I am, no problem, dear Daphne will tell me.

There are only three possible attitudes your customer can have, and she can only hold one of those attitudes at any one time. If the attitude is acceptance, she'll sign the cheque. If it is still objection, she will object and you know how to handle objections. If she shows indifference, if she wants to "go home and think about it," then you are ready to probe, to try and discover areas of discomfort or areas of need that you can work on.

If you just aren't sure what attitude they hold, there is only one thing to do. You have nothing to lose by trying to close. It is much better than: "Umm, err, well, err, I don't really know what to do now, err, would you like to think about it?"

Another old favourite of mine!

18

SHOOT TO KILL

How many of you have got a brood of youngsters?

Picture the scene, it is Sunday morning around lunchtime. Ever since she rose and shone, the lady of the house has been cooking up a culinary treat, as well as dropping a hint or two that you may like to join her in the world of the awake and working.

You have dragged yourself out of bed and have just got enough energy left over from the energy-sapping act of getting shaved and dressed for a day of leisure, to stagger downstairs, pour yourself a coffee and make it to the lounge, before dropping exhausted into your favourite easy chair.

About this time, your four-year-old bounces into the room and, from a good six feet away, she launches herself like an American footballer about to dive a touchdown, landing right where it makes your eyes water. Boy did you need that.

Wife meanwhile, toiling amongst the boiling broccoli, suggests that you may like to look at her car, which is making funny noises again. You slump down a little, hoping that if you can't see her, she'll believe that you have gone away. Your eyes stagger around the room, looking for the Sunday paper; there it is on the doormat about twelve feet away. The way you feel, it may as well be on top of Everest.

You search for help. Four-year-old is winding herself up to spring again so you try a diversionary tactic: "Pass Daddy his paper, darling."

It doesn't work. With the most evil of grins she dives again, forcing you to roll out of the way. She misses. You try again: 'My newspaper – pleease." Off she goes, all the way to the door in one bound of pure energy and she's back, climbing all over your shoulders and tearing great lumps out of the pin-up before whirling outside, like some tropical tempest, to join the older two and start up the day's hostilities.

You slide lower down in your chair and begin your holiday diet of stories about vicars, choirboys, stepladders and tubs of strawberry yoghurt. Those journalists get more imaginative every week. You have just got to the juicy bit and she's back.

You didn't even see her and there she is all over your knee; the sound of crumpled newspaper fills your ears. You are not happy. Then she says: "Give me a biscuit dad?"

"Not unless you ask properly."

"Please can I have a biscuit, dad?"

"Oh, no sorry, look at the time, you'll spoil your Sunday lunch."

Have any of you got a youngster who will answer that perfectly reasonable refusal with: "O.K. daddy, I'll go out to play again then, and leave you in peace."

You haven't, have you? They don't say that, do they? They say: "Oh go on daddy, let me have a biscuit, you said I could, please daddy, just one, go on, I said please, it won't spoil my lunch, it won't, it won't..."

You bat gamely on with: "I've said no. It's just before lunch and you're not having a biscuit."

"It's not fair... you said that if I said please... I'm not your friend. I want a biscuit." She raises her voice, stamps her feet and begins to wail.

You are still speaking quietly, trying to remain invisible from the attentions of wife. You murmur: "You're not having a biscuit and that's final, go away, I'm trying to read my paper." Then the bottom lip comes out and you know you're in trouble. It is amazing how such little people can cause so much pandemonium.

There is only one thing left for you to do. You stand up raise yourself to your full height and in your most authoritative tones you say: "Here, you can have one. But just one, mind. Don't tell your brother and sister and don't you dare tell your mum!"

She's got her way, she has sold you on the idea of giving her a biscuit. She has used an effective technique which, in the hands of "little horror", was irresistible. That technique was "persistence." She asked, and when you objected she ignored your objection and she closed again, and again, and again until she got what she wanted.

What am I suggesting? That if customer refuses to buy, you stamp your feet, tear your clothes and hold your breath until your face goes blue. Well, yes, if it works do that.

It happened to me once, I told this particular salesman, whom I'd known for some years, that I was about to remove his goods from display and replace them with another brand. He went berserk. Told me it wasn't fair, he went on and on about all the work he'd done organising the displays in the first place. He looked so distressed that I felt sorry for him. And because of that I changed my mind and replaced the goods with new models from his range. Very similar technique to that employed by young Melanie.

If that method's not for you, think of this aspect. There's an old saying in selling – "it's the squeaky gate that gets oiled." This usually refers to those folk with complaints who ring you with loud and regular anger, trying to ensure that you solve their problem before you set to work on someone else's. But it could also refer to the salespeople, who patiently and regularly put themselves in front of their customers and always ask for some commitment to buy, rather than letting prospect off by not asking!

Absolute persistence will buy you a lot of meals. Keep at it as long as necessary. If you do, you are bound to be successful. No-one has failed until they stopped trying!

The Al Capone method
The thing about absolute persistence is that as you end up seeing people many many times, eventually you may find yourself running out of things to say to them. So perhaps you should consider ways of making that dogged persistence more effective.

Have you ever had a customer who tells you that he wants your goods, but not yet? Some customers don't seem to realise that there is some urgency to this selling game. You have to eat every day. It's no fun starving for a month or two, secure in the knowledge that there is a banquet coming. You need to be prepared with something that will persuade customer to buy – NOW.

Imagine yourself to be a gangster, deeply committed to protection rackets. Your living comes from persuading the owners of small businesses to give you a share of their takings in exchange for the promise that their persons and premises won't be remodelled by your local thugs!

You show your victims due respect, walk quietly into their

"Excuse me please, I'm a racketeer..."

place of business, and politely say: "Excuse me please, I'm a racketeer, will you hand over half of the money in your till?"

The businessman will most probably phone the boys in blue, who will invite you to spend a few years under Her Majesty's care. You needed more. You needed something to persuade the businessman to act out of character – to give you the money that he had worked hard for.

Unfortunately, on this occasion you didn't have that "something" so now you have some time on your hands – about ten years less remission for good behaviour! You decide to use that time to study your particular problem and find a solution.

When your ten years are up, you try again. You walk up to your victim but this time, you pull out a shotgun, point it at the victim and politely say: "Excuse me please, but I'm a racketeer, give me some money."

This time the businessman reacts rather differently. And you become very wealthy. You have found a way of prompting that businessman into immediate action. You produced a gun. I can think of a lot of my old prospective customers that I would have liked to use a gun on, unfortunately it isn't the sort of equipment that we salespeople can use.

Apart from the fact that they would bleed all over our Gucci shoes, if we shot our customers they would never pay up. But like the racketeer we ought to have something. Something that persuades customer to buy now! Today! This minute! Something that persuades him not to go home and think about it.

What that something is depends upon what you are selling. If you are a retailer it could be a special offer; interest-free credit; winter, spring, summer or autumn sales; whatever, all for a limited period only. This exercise gives you the chance to have a little fun, and to use some imagination. Keep the offers honest, otherwise you lay yourself open to accusations of being a conman, as well as to the attentions of the Office of

Fair Trading and the consumer protection organisations.

I know there are salespeople around who abuse this technique. Some of the methods I have heard of include one chap who was selling furniture – to order. He used this "bullet" in his gun:

Whenever he had a customer who told him they wanted to buy, but they couldn't give him the business just yet, he would suggest to them that it was an awful pity that they couldn't, because he needed just two more orders to make up a container load. If he could order a complete container full he would be given an extra 5% discount by the manufacturer.

He told his prospect that he had someone coming to see him that afternoon to place the other order and that if they could order today – then he would pass that 5% on to them. Sometimes, his customer was persuaded to place their order, there and then. Mostly they saw through his ruse, and said uncomplimentary things about him to their friends!

If you are selling to industry, your "shotgun" may be a promotion or a competition, aimed at giving the buyer a perk, or the old favourite a pending price increase. The best ammunition for your shotgun is that which is tuned to appeal directly to your target. The individual customer.

Even when genuine offers are used as the ammunition for your "shotgun", some salesmen have difficulty accepting that they are ethical methods; that's up to you. But don't feel too sorry for your customers. They seem to be very adept at dreaming up reasons why they are not ready to buy just yet, some of which aren't even close to the truth.

If you can use your imagination and knowledge of your particular industry to find the kind of ammunition that suits your own code of ethics, then that's perfect. But don't go in with a water pistol if the competition has a missile launcher. You'll look a right drip.

19

FOLLOW UP ACTION

The easiest sale you will ever make is a sale introduced by referral! Whatever you're selling, if your customer has had praise for you and your product enthused onto his doubting ear-drums by one whom he trusts and respects, then the cheque is already filled in before you even get face to face. You just need to get customer to autograph it.

Referrals are money in the bank so let's look at ways to earn them.

Earning a referral
Most salespeople believe that their job ends when they see the soles of their customers' dainty feet tripping happily out of their showroom. It gives them a peaceful warmth, to think that they now have time to pop the kettle on and mentally relax after the cut and thrust of a spirited sales presentation.

But that's dead wrong.

If you want repeat business, either in the form of another order from dear departing customer, or from someone to whom that customer recommends you, then the days following the sale are the prime time to achieve that recommendation. There are two different ways that it works.

Lead time
First case is when there is a lead time, between the customer

placing the order with you, and your receiving the goods from
your suppliers, or being able to deliver to customer.

The very best referrals come in this period. It's the time
when customers are warmed up with anticipation and
excitement at the prospect of playing with their new
purchase. They will talk enthusiastically to their friends and
family, telling everyone how nice you are, what great value
for money they're getting and how excited they are at the
prospect to be enjoyed. Doesn't matter whether they're
buying a new car, a washing machine or home computer, this
is the time, before they've even set their hands on the goods,
that they could be working really well for you.

It is the perfect time for you to motivate your customer into
even greater efforts; it's the time for you to look for every
possible excuse to pick up the phone and enthuse to them
about their purchase.

And I mean any excuse. If you can phone every day with
good news, if you can share and heighten their anticipation,
these few days will be time well spent. Customer won't be
used to such service, you'll become bosom buddies.

What could you phone about? Say they've bought a
washing machine, your call could be: "Hello Mrs. Prospect,
I've got some great news... we have had confirmation from
the warehouse to say that your machine has come into stock
three days early... the manufacturer has just been on to say
that your machine will be with us this week, rather than next
Wednesday. Shall I organise delivery for Thursday?... I
spoke to the plumber for you and he can come round with
your new machine, tomorrow morning, if that suits you...
the *Which* report has just cited your new machine as best of
breed." Anything that constitutes good news, share it with
customer.

There is another good reason to give them a call at this
time; if they have been spreading the word about how good
you are, human nature being what it is, one of the recipients
of that news may be feeling a little jealous. Maybe they talk to

brother-in-law. He's an expert on washing machines. As well as anything else you care to mention.

He's made a few spiked comments like: "I suppose it's got an 1500 rpm spin speed," and "For that price it must have a stainless steel drum and tub?" And: "Our machine has an all wool program." And: "What about the liquid detergent dispenser, does it have one built in?"

Perhaps Mr. and Mrs. Customer don't know the answers to these points. They've put a deposit on your machine and are beginning to feel somewhat nervous. Yesterday they were praising you like there was money in it for them, today they've gone really quiet.

Phone at this time and you might run into some straight questioning. But nothing you can't answer, and you'll have the perfect opportunity to put their minds at rest and get them talking again.

After delivery

Trying that little bit harder gets you a nose ahead of the opposition. Customer contact once the sale is made is just the thing to put you top in the "little bit harder" stakes. So does the "how are you getting on with it?" call just after they've taken delivery. I'm thinking of those purchases I made when the modern technology left me scratching my head and wondering what was this monster I'd just bought.

Funnily enough my first such monster was a fully-automatic washing machine, made in Italy. At last my wife and I could forgo the weekly trip down to the laundrette and have our clothes washed in the comfort of our own kitchen. We were so excited by our new washer that as soon as the plumber left, we set two stools in front of our shiny new purchase to watch it perform, and switched it on. This alone was quite a feat, after two hours trying to decipher the Italian turned to English from the little booklet, anyway at last we'd done it.

Behind the glass door, all the water was wooshing around, mixed amongst it was a coloured pile of our best garments.

... we set two stools in front of our shiny new purchase to watch it perform.

Time passed and the sound of running water tuned our attention to the soap dispenser. Wondering if the machine had taken in all the soap, I pulled it open. Instantly the kitchen floor was covered in water. This couldn't be right. It was supposed to wash clothes, not the floor.

I tried again, same result. I phoned the shop. "Leave the soap dispenser alone," they said. I did. It stopped wetting the floor and we all lived happily ever after.

Even on something as simple as a washing machine, I could have been so impressed by a salesperson who phoned to ask how I was doing. Impressed enough to recommend anyone I knew to buy from that salesperson. Washing machine salesperson missed the opportunity.

Then came the micro-computer! Anybody got one? The thing is, when you're talking to an animate object, like a human being or a dog, and it isn't doing what you're telling it to do, you can use the force of your personality to persuade, cajole or bully it to conform to your will. Even when you're in the wrong. You can even do this with some inanimate objects. Not computers though!

They're such clever little sparks. You do what it says in the book, expecting wondrous things to happen and it says things like: "File not found." "Disc fault 18 at :0 28/05" or "Mistake". You can shout and curse and tell it 'til you're blue in the gills that you are right and it is wrong, but it keeps coming up with: "File not found..."

And there's nobody around to protect you from it. You are all alone with a manual the size of a bible which talks a language one step removed from Latin. Like: "Decrement ROM polling semaphore." Anyone know what that means? Well don't tell me, I'm not interested. Instead turn yourself into a computer salesman, follow up all your sales with a "have you figured out how to switch it on yet?" phone call, and you'll have so many computer customers eating out of your hand you'll have to set up crowd barriers. Believe me, I know!

As for the shop who sold me mine, they were too busy to bother with even the most rudimentary training that I tell people not to go there, because they don't care. I looked for another dealer who did care about me. I buy their floppy disks and send all my friends in to buy their hardware. Recommends come in two forms, positive and negative.

When you do phone, and after you have told them how to use the beast, ask customer for a name or two; you aren't being nice for nothing. The best way to get referrals is ... you guessed it ... to ask for them. Don't let this opportunity pass.

Send a thank you note

Back to departing customer. Have you ever sent a past customer a thank you note? Have you ever received a "thank you for buying off me" note, from a salesman? If you have, then you have dealt with a star. Here's what I mean.

Say you sell holidays. The Tanner family have just been on one of your sundrenched sessions at the Spanish seaside. The week following their return they receive a "thank you" card, one of the birthday card style, with an appropriate illustration on the front, and inside you have added a short message, scripted in your own fair hand. It goes something like:

"Thanks for going on holiday with us. I hope you had a great time."

You sign it. With your Christian name. It's not from the company. It is a personal note from you.

It will be the first time anyone in the Tanner family has ever received a greetings card without having a Birthday. Greetings cards mean a lot to people. These cards have warm personal messages on them, they always make us feel good, they let us know that somebody loves us. We put them on the top of the telly for all to see. Perhaps Mr. and Mrs. Tanner's friends or family will see it and ask whose birthday they've forgotten. The Tanners can't help but feel good, your name must get a mention.

You just need to be a nose ahead, remember?

Then, as soon as the new brochures come out for next year's holidays, or if you happen to have some weekend breaks or end of season bargains, you can post them another personal note along with the details. You send them greetings cards, you are their friend, as soon as they want a holiday, they'll be in to see you.

Give a little

You sell cars. Nigel and Edwina Teararound have just bought their third fastback from you in four years. You have a record of their purchases, you have sent them some: "I like you," notes to keep your name in the forefront of their minds, but now you really want to cement the relationship, now's the time for a small gift. Nothing expensive, you aren't trying to bribe them, just a small token of your thanks.

Again a day or two after they have taken delivery, drop in on them with a parcel, say a set of seat covers or floor mats, or wheel trims, nothing too fancy. It is a token of your appreciation for their business, just hand it over and say:

"You have just bought your third car from me and you have been a pleasure to deal with each time. I would like you to have this small gift as a personal token of my thanks." You and them, no sales pitch, no "I hope you'll buy number four", no request for referrals. Just a gift because you enjoyed doing business with them.

People who enjoy doing business with you will want to share the pleasure with their friends, they will spread your name around everyone they know. Prospects will flood in.

I know one company. They are called G. Clifford Morris, they sell plumbing materials. Unfortunately I do not sell plumbing materials, at least not many. Their representative calls about once a quarter. A week before he calls I receive a letter, it goes like this:-

Dear Mr. Moss

On Friday next, the 25th March, Mr. Bruce F. Brian will have the great pleasure of calling upon you.

If you could find it possible to see our Representative when he calls, this would be considered a very special favour.

It is always our good fortune to call upon you.

Your sincerely

Of all the companies I deal with, G. Clifford Morris are the only ones who do this, and it doesn't end there. When Friday comes, and Bruce calls, the first thing he does is give me some presents; good quality ball-points, bulldog clips, carrier bags and coasters to cover the coffee rings on my desk where I set my mug down. All these items are overprinted with G. Clifford Morris's name and address and it doesn't end there. The other thing this company sends are cards printed with famous sayings of wisdom, or poems. I love to receive mail-outs and visits from Mr. Morris's company.

Every time Bruce calls I try to find something to buy from him, every time I need anything remotely related to plumbing, I phone him first. I am almost desperate to do business with a company that is so nice. Just lately they've started to stock a product which I use a lot. No prizes for guessing whom I'll buy that product from!

Prospecting for repeat business is as simple as being considerate and genuinely nice to people.

Action to iron out snags

Ever had a service problem to sort out? The type where customer claims that one of the thermostatic radiator valves, which you sold them, started to leak, and they couldn't shut it off, and it was wetting the carpet, so husband decided to remove the radiator, to take it round to the plumber, to get the valve fixed, but in doing so he emptied the whole central heating system, through the ceiling of their lounge, which is ruined, and covered the real cow hide settee plus the Bang and Wallop stereo system, plus the television and video recorder, and the best Wilton, with that disgusting, mucky brown stuff that seeps out of central heating radiators and it's all your fault and what are you going to do about it?

What's your reaction? "Don't be a berk. It's not my fault, your husband shouldn't have messed about with it in the first place!" Well so he shouldn't, I mean I do know that customers bring half these troubles on themselves. But on some occasions they have a genuine complaint and even when it's a 50/50 case, a little extra effort can actually end up by turning that service problem into a good thing!

In such situations you can look on customer complaints as another great opportunity to make a real friend who buys from you time and time again. You could actually finish up welcoming complaint calls.

To be totally mercenary, I should say that those occasions are the ones where it will only cost you a small amount of money to hang on to customer's goodwill. I'm not suggesting that you spend a fortune, you don't need to; often a bouquet of flowers with a "sorry to hear about your trouble" card will do.

Perhaps a visit from you, along with someone from the manufacturer, to make sure of the cause of the complaint and that it is rectified, will be sufficient. It may be worthwhile replacing the items in question for a completely new set. There is no sense in digging your heels in, if the customer is not being unreasonable, and if only a small amount of money is involved.

If it is their new car that's broken something vital, lend them a better one until it's fixed. If their new cooker has blown a gasket, take them out for a meal.

When you think about your insurance cover and the real cost of such actions, after the tax people have had their share, allied to the fact that you can enjoy that meal with them, plus their future business and recommendations, you may end up earning money, as well as referrals, from complaints. Don't get bogged down trying to prove you're in the right, it could cost you all that.

Our willingness to put effort into following up our sales should take into account that it is the single most effective guarantee of ensuring our sales for tomorrow.

20

MASTERING THE BLOWER

You are a plumber. You're standing in the queue at the local builders' merchants hoping that they have got the sprogget in stock that will raise you out of the mire and persuade your meanest customer to love you again.

Was it your fault that he chose that type of boiler? Were you supposed to tell him that if the sprogget broke (which has been known to happen), they were very difficult to obtain? You don't think you were wrong. You think that the only thing you did wrong was to sell something to the psychopathic ape in the first place.

He's built like a block of flats. He thinks you should have told him what might happen. He says that if you can't mend the leaks in his new boiler by tonight, your doctor's going to be mending you before sunrise. Boy, do you need that sprogget.

You've been standing patiently in the queue for at least ten minutes. Why don't they get more staff? Why are this dozy lot so slow? The lump of impatience that started in your chest has just about reached your throat. By God they'd better have that sprogget after this wait. You are feeling hot.

At last it's your turn. As soon as this bozo stops writing on that tiny bit of paper, looks up and says: "Who's next?" you will be in, he will have the sprogget, he will put you out of your misery. You hope.

He looks up. You stand to attention. He asks: "Who'
next?" You bristle and surge forward. The phone on the wal
rings, he turns on his heels and goes to answer it. You collaps
on the floor in a big shaking heap.

It's just not fair. You have waited patiently for the best par
of a quarter of an hour, nerves a jingle, to see if you could b
saved from King Kong. The bloke he's talking to now, jus
twiddled his fingers, rung a little bell and he's being served
The telephone is that powerful.

It is a power that can make your life a misery, but it is also
power that you can use to your own advantage. Like al
things of power, accepted ways of use have grown up over th
years, mythical rules which must be obeyed.

Myth number one – It must be answered with all haste. Thi
first rule is founded on fear, the fear of missing something, th
ache of wondering who it was, if you do miss it.

Myth number two – To be successful in telephone selling yo
must be fully prepared at all times.

Myth number three – Once you have answered the phone yo
cannot escape listening. You may be getting the roasting o
your life from someone standing miles away, yet it i
impossible to put that receiver down until the caller ha
finished. It is the height of rudeness and is bound to destro
all goodwill.

Myth number four – You are honour-bound to respond to it
call. Even if you are out when caller first tries, he can leave hi
name and number and you are bound to call him back. If yo
are expecting an irate phone caller to nail you, you can spen
most of the day biting your finger nails, trying to avoid th
inevitable contact.

Myth number five – The caller has first opportunity to contro
what happens next. He has the authority of summoning yo
to join in a conversation, he is prepared and knows what h
wants to say. Caller will always steal the initiative an

command the situation. It is always better to be the caller than the callee.

For all salespeople the telephone is unavoidable, to many it can be a nightmare. Handled with skill it can be an invaluable piece of kit. Let's see how you can master it.

Myth number 1

It must be answered with all haste. Obviously, to a professional salesman trying to stay one step ahead of his opposition, all phone calls must be regarded as an opportunity to sell and must be dealt with. So myth number 1 looks as if it holds up to examination. Except you are going to control this insistent little device just as if it were a wayward pet that needed some discipline.

You answer the phone when it suits you. If you are sitting making chains out of paper clips than a chat on the phone will be most welcome, if however you are up to your toupee in calculations working on your plans for a tricky sales presentation, trying hard to concentrate, then a ringing in your ears is the last thing you want.

You might have a secretary, or a willing spouse. If that's the case then you can declare "quiet time" to cover your mental gymnastics. Quiet time is simply time set aside when you are not available to answer the phone.

If you feel awkward about it you can instruct secretary to say that you are "out" or "with a client" or, the strongest one, "in a meeting". Secretary takes name and number and you phone them back when quiet time is over. But "not available to answer phone calls until after 11.30," will suffice.

I know several companies who have "quiet times" at set periods of the day, between 9.30 and 11.30 for instance. Regular callers soon get used to avoiding these times, just as they get used to avoiding calling during the lunch hour. It is my personal belief that much more work would be processed if industry agreed set periods of "quiet time" during the week for paperwork to be handled without the constant interruption of the telephone.

If there is no secretary and the spouse has a headache, then you can turn to technology for assistance: the dreaded answerphone. If people don't like using the phone, and most folk don't, nobody likes answerphones. Almost all replies to answerphone messages go something like this: "Aw bother . . . click . . . brrrrrrrrrrrr."

But they are a very useful device, so what can you do to encourage your reluctant callers to use them? Answerphone messages are usually very formal. "This is Howard I Dooit, the plumber speaking, the office is not manned at the moment, please leave your name, number and your message after the tone – beep . . . beep . . . beep."

Too heavy; folk feel very foolish talking to themselves and a machine. If you're going to use an answerphone keep your requests for information light.

How about: "Hello this is Howard Dooit, just leave your number and name on this machine and I'll phone you back – beep . . . beep . . . beep." It shouldn't be too hard for caller to stutter out his name and number, and if he wants to, he'll leave a message. If that doesn't work for you, try something else and keep trying until more people talk to you than ring off.

Just in case these first two escape routes don't work for you, there is a third. There are many firms in this country now who will run an answering service for you. You pay so much per week and they take your calls. All you have to do is call in each day for your messages and then contact those who sought your ear.

It will cost you money but then so will constant interruptions, or missed enquiries because you weren't there. Come to that, so would the car phone that goes off in the middle of some delicate manoeuvre and causes you to remodel your motor, or worse!!

So Myth 1 bites the dust. You answer when it suits you best, but don't miss the business.

Myth number two

To be successful at converting telephone enquiries into sales you must be fully prepared at all times.

Amongst other things, telephones are designed to ring only when you're not ready. It is 9 o'clock in the morning, you are sitting comfortably at your desk, chin cupped gently in your palm trying to recover from the trauma of getting out of bed. IT rings. You jolt in surprise, your elbow slips off the desk-top, your chin drops hard against the receiver launching it high into the air. You make a mad grab for it and tip boiling coffee down your suit trousers.

"Hello." IT says, "I'm ringing about your ad. in the evening paper."

You think: "Ad., what ad.? Did we have a special offer? What was it, where's that paper?" You look down and notice that you have just mopped your trousers dry with the very information that this chap is seeking.

Your brain stops, there is no way it's going to get involved in this debacle. You panic, you go from totally mute to babbling incoherently and very fast. Your voice climbs a few decibels as the speed of your speech increases – words just splurge out.

You have to press on, silence would be deafening, in less than a minute you have told the caller all you know. Caller thanks you and hangs up, never to be heard from again. You stand up, walk over to the wall and begin banging your head against it. It wasn't fair, you were caught by surprise. You weren't ready.

There isn't a salesperson alive who is ever ready for the phone *and* is doing business, so what can you do to be ready the next time the phone rings?

Let's start by examining what is running through the mind of the caller as he wakes you out of your mid-morning torpor. Whether he knows it or not, there are certain set ideas in his mind when he phones you, and he will try very hard to see those ideas through. All callers follow a familiar pattern.

He wants to buy

The good news is that he does want to buy your product. He was interested enough to read your ad., he has made the effort to note down the number and he has rung you up. As I said earlier, most people dislike telephones; to some people this dislike can become a phobia. For anyone, phoning around, speaking to strangers is not exactly fun.

So when somebody does ring your bell asking questions about the goods that you are selling, he wants some. That's the good news, that makes telephone training worth pursuing.

However, the process which we all go through before we buy, follows these lines: First, list down all the possible alternatives which may fulfil your needs. You make as long a list as you can and you get all excited at the thought of following up on every one of them. You rush round to see the products you have listed and as soon as you do, the emphasis reverses. Now you feel a desperate urge to cull that list down to the few alternatives which will make your decision-making easier.

Out come the "what-ifs": What if I can't really afford it?; What if I'm made redundant next week?; What if I buy it and then see one cheaper somewhere else?; What if this model is a Friday afternoon special and is nothing but trouble?; What if this salesman is ripping me off?; What if I smash my new car up, get laid up in hospital, lose my job, the wreckage gets repossessed by the finance house, the police discover my insurance has just run out and I spend the rest of my days in prison? What-ifs aren't always rational, but they are damned good at stopping us from buying.

We all dislike taking the responsibility for buying something and feel a strong need to get the process over with, by cutting our list down, as quickly as possible. Sometimes we eliminate all the items from our list and put off the buying to another day.

It's just the same on the phone. Prospect's top priority, when he first calls you, will be to find a good reason to eliminate you from the list. He will ask awkward questions in the hope that you will go in full throttle and slam straight into this ambush. If you do that, you will never get the chance to see how ugly he is.

Understanding caller's mental menu enables you to prepare your own strategy, to turn this motivated prospect into next week's supply of brown ale and chips.

Set an appointment

Because you cannot be prepared for a phone enquiry, you need to have a clear objective that you wish to achieve whenever someone calls you in response to an advert. You have spent money putting your advert in the paper, you may as well make the effort to capitalise on that money now that you have the opportunity.

The sole objective has to be to sell the goods. Unfortunately I can't do that over the phone; I've even tried straightening out the curly wire so that caller could see through it and eyeball my wares, but to no avail. I don't think caller was

I've even tried straightening out the curly wire...

really trying! Anyhow, for me, selling on the phone doesn't work, so I revised my objective to that of setting an appointment.

Caller's objective may be to ask lots of questions in order to get you to eliminate yourself from his list of possibilities, yours is to get him in to see you. Everything you say should be tuned to those objectives.

You can prepare yourself by creating questions that will encourage the caller to keep talking to you. Ask questions that give you the maximum opportunity to listen to what he has to say.

You need to develop an affinity with the caller. He will only come in to see you if he feels that it will benefit him to do so. Simply trying to tell him that he will benefit doesn't work, everyone he calls will be telling him that. You have to be smarter than the average. Instead of telling, ask. Ask him open questions, which let him know that you may have information that he doesn't possess.

Questions such as:- "Have you experienced the clarity of our latest compact disc players?" – "Have you had a test drive in the new, active suspension Vauxette SRi?" – "When did you last have your vision tested by our laser optometry computer?" – don't tell him anything that he can fall out with. Such questions rather suggest that you know something which is worth finding out about, they are designed to make him curious, about compact discs; active suspension; laser optometry. Curiosity is a great motivator.

But the best question of all for setting an appointment is: "Let me put aside some time especially for you. Is this afternoon okay or will tomorrow morning suit you better?"

Funny thing about asking for an appointment, the more you ask, the more you are likely to get an appointment to sell.

Let's look at some other questions specifically designed to turn telephone enquiries into appointments. You ought to have a whole list of them, which you stick onto the face of the phone so that you are ready to go when next it surprises you.

It doesn't matter what those questions are, so long as they aim toward your objective – setting an appointment.

Here is the first one:

Telephone: "Ring. Ring."

Us: "Hello."

Prospect: "Hello, I'm ringing about your ad. in the Towncentre Trumpet."

Us: "Ah yes. Will you read the advert out for me please?"

This has to be the all-time best opening question in answer to an ad. call. It gives you three valuable assets:

Time; the phone call shocked you out of your favourite daydream, the one about the Isle of Capri. While the caller reads out the ad. you have time to return to the real world.

Information; if you listen carefully, the caller just may let slip some information that will help you attain your objective. You wrote the ad., so you know it off by heart, but just now is the time to let customer hold centre stage, resist all temptation to butt in and help them with this small task because the third thing this question gives you is:-

Control; You cannot sell the goods if you lose control of the situation. On the phone you are caught out, caller has the initiative. Asking direct questions, which persuade caller to do your bidding, will regain you that initiative and give you control of the dealings. Control must be gained gently, in small doses which should begin the instant you lift that receiver.

Caller reads: "It says you have an Atari 520 STFM home computer at £279.95."

Us: "Yes, go on. We have several ads. running and I want to be sure I have the right one. Read me the whole ad. please."

Caller will do it. He wants the information, he can't eliminate you unless he has enough information. And you have taken the first steps towards gaining control.

Question number two gains you the initiative: "What was it about the advert that specifically caught your eye?"

People buy for their reasons, not ours. It is much easier to succeed if you know what their reason for calling is.

Perhaps your ad. read:-

Home Computer – Atari 520 STFM – Mouse – Disc drive – 52k memory – shocking pink casing – £279.95.

That's five features including the price. Caller could have been attracted by any of these features but chances are it is only one of them that has turned him on. He tells you that he has wanted a home computer for a long time, he would have bought one last year if only they had had shocking pink casings. All the other features are very interesting but it has to be pink!

You may think he's a little weird but this is no time to share that thought with him. Support him. Agree with his good taste. Compliment him on his discerning view of colour. Tell him how that pink case will contribute to his enjoyment of the Atari. Forget all about the other features and restrict the conversation to the areas of his interest, he'll love you for it. How can he eliminate someone he loves?

Question three is the last one that's mandatory: "Can we arrange to meet this afternoon or is tomorrow better?"

Go for the appointment. You've earned it, the worst he can say is "clear off" and you should expect about a quarter of callers to suggest that. That's why you need lots and lots more questions – to keep them talking until they change their attitude and rush round to buy.

Asking for the appointment should feature heavily on your list of questions, it ought to be question number 3 and then number 5, 7, 9, 11 and on and on until he says yes or finally hangs up on you. The more you ask, the more you get. Get asking.

So myth number two, to be successful you must be fully prepared at all times, has some truth to it. But that preparation can only consist of a clear telephone objective and a pre-planned list of questions to help you on your way.

Myth number three

Once you have answered the phone you cannot escape listening, true or false?

Remember ape? Well, last time, you fixed his boiler, he didn't tear parts of you off. But this morning he has rung up again. He wants to know when his new bath is being delivered. You told him that you would ring supplier for a delivery date and phone him back during the afternoon, only something else cropped up and you forgot to ring supplier.

Now he's got you, he is on the phone and both of you know he expects his answer. On the phone it is far better to be the caller than the callee, so how are you going to do it, how are you going to gain control in this situation?

Myth says you can't, not without losing goodwill. I say you can, and it's not that difficult. Simply cut yourself off. I don't mean ring off, that's likely to bring ape's wrath roaring round to plant tyre tracks on your nose end. What I do mean is to carry on speaking but hang up while you are half way through a senten ... brrrrrrrrrrrrrr.

He doesn't know it was you who did it, I mean people don't cut themselves off while they are talking, that's down to Telecom or a dozy secretary or some such. There's no goodwill lost in being cut off. Instantly you phone supplier and find the info that will placate him.

If he phones back, that's okay, you will be engaged, trying to phone him back! You can leave the phone off the hook for a while if you need more time, you got cut off didn't you? Perhaps there's a fault on the line. Ape doesn't know and you have won some time to gather your thoughts before you ring back.

Then when you are ready, call him back. Now you are the caller, now you have all the information at your fingertips, now you are surprising him. You have regained control. Don't do it too often, you'll get sussed out, but being conveniently cut off while someone is dumping their displeasure down your ear is a great way of levelling the myth that says you can't terminate a call without being rude. You just have.

Myth number four
You are honour-bound to respond to the telephone's call. If you want repeat business then this one stands up. Again you can pick your time, except the best time to phone them back is just before they phone you again. This one gives you a golden opportunity to shine in their eyes. One of the biggest moans heard in business today is: "They never phone back."

Make sure you do and jump one step ahead.

Myth number five
The caller has first opportunity to control the conversation. We've almost covered this with our questions to gain control; you can do it on the phone (but it takes very good balance!). What helps most in this situation is a calm and authoritative tone of voice.

Don't apologise unnecessarily, don't get angry. The phone will always make you sound more blunt than you normally are, same for the caller, perhaps he doesn't quite mean it like it sounds on the phone.

If you are in the wrong, and caller does deserve an apology, then give him one. Don't blame your supplier for the cock-up, don't blame your colleagues, or your company, take the blame on yourself. There is no finer way of taking the sting out of caller's complaint than admitting that it was all your own fault. Nobody does that either; you will shock him into silence and be able to command the situation.

A telephone appointment
A final quicky for those salespeople who earn their living selling to professional buyers, especially the ones with secretaries who always insist that prospect is out or demand to know your name, rank and serial number before they will

allow you to pass through their protective screen and accost the ears of the person who just might be interested in buying your stuff.

You have all experienced it:-

Rep: "Is Bruce Buyalot in please?"

Secretary: "Who is speaking?"

Rep: "It's Flogger Bentgear, may I speak to Bruce."

Secretary: "I'm afraid he's not in at the moment, if you would like to tell me what it's about, I will relate your message to Mr Buyalot and get him to call you back if he's interested."

Flogger isn't likely to get an appointment through this guardian angel, she might be good with a typewriter, but she's not a patch on Flogger when it comes to persuading people to buy his goods. He needs a lever to winkle her out of the game.

Flogger has one, he simply says: "I'm sorry that won't be possible, you see I plan my work from a forward looking filofax so I can't let you know where to reach me, I'll have to call you back. When will Mr. Buyalot be in?"

He has winkled her, she won't have a clue what a forward looking filofax is. Brucie won't have a clue what a forward looking filofax is, not even Flogger knows. But she won't ask, she will simply comply with his question and leave her boss open to Flogger's silver tongue.

The terror of the telephone can be tamed. All it needs is a little understanding, a good technique and more than a touch of cunning. That's all.

21

STAY SELLING – STAY SANE

The day begins badly. A sales meeting with the purple-faced fiend who rants and raves around the corridors of your workplace. The sales director! He is after blood. He says that to call your discussion a sales meeting is to mis-describe it, that to be a sales meeting it had to be about sales. You had nothing to tell him!

All that day you smile, chat, generate enough nervous energy to fill in a page or two of your order book, enough to ward off the fiend for a while.

Now, you've finished. You are back in the car, sitting outside your last call of the day. Before you turn the ignition, you enjoy a few minutes of peace and quiet. The adrenalin you have lived on all day, ceases to pump. Your thoughts are beginning to experience great difficulty forcing their way through the old grey cells. Your eyes start to look inwards. There's only one thing left to do. You let out a huge sigh and turn from work-mode into zombie-mode, ready for home.

Pretty soon you will wind down even further, into slob-mode. The motor steers itself onto your drive. Boy, is the car door heavy tonight? You slouch up the path, silently step inside, hoping that you can get your coat off before the kids hear you, or better still that they've gone to bed.

Time for the second sigh. This one heralds the rush of complaints you are going to pour out onto your spouse, you work on the premise that you have to get in there first, so partner won't hit you with a task to do, too early in the game. You believe that an evening shrouded in silence, ogling the drivel that pours out of the box, is what you need!

You believe that everyone is entitled to half an hour of complete calm when they come home, to help them make the switch from worker to doting parent and spouse.

But what does dear wife say to this form of home-coming. Is it: "Oh I am sorry to hear that. Come on over here honey, let me help you put your feet up. Do you want your favourite telly programme on, your dinner's almost ready. I'll just go and get it for you, would you like the chilled white or a red?"

Do the children hover obediently by the door, smiling quietly, waiting for you weakly to beckon them over one by one for a chaste kiss. Is that what happens? Is it *****!

Wife hits you with: "It's no good you expecting dinner to be ready, while you've been sitting, swanning around in that car all day, I've had one hell of a time! Lucy put the baby in the spin dryer and he's been at hospital all afternoon with dizzy spells. Not only that but on the way home the engine fell out of my old banger, you will have to look at it for me. Oh, that reminds me, the washer's making that funny noise again, like it did when Jonathan washed his bike wheels. Can you take a squint at it when you've fixed the car? Do you want me to go to the take-away or will you?"

The kids, meanwhile, hit you with everything they've got and then want to eat your dinner for you; one of them perched precariously on your left shoulder, where she can drop her half-chewed chip down the back of your neck. The other two are leaning over the arms of your easy chair, fighting each other to get between your fork and your face!

That's the way it is with families, and some days that's just not much fun. Is it? So what should you do? You have to find some way to relieve the tension, you can't go around all your life with the pressure building up inside. If you do, you'll have so much steam pouring out of your ears, you'll strip off the

... you'll strip off the wall paper as you walk past.

wall paper as you walk past, and give yourself another job to tackle!

Like all other aspects of selling, the cure is not hard, in fact it's quite fun. It might be something which you find a little strange but I'm going to suggest it anyway! I'm going to suggest that it is part of the job of every salesman and saleswoman – it is part of your job to make one extra business call every day, always to the same place always selling the same thing to the same people.

You sell yourself as a parent to the kiddies and as loving spouse to your dearest. It will take no more than half an hour a day and the value of the income will be immeasurable.

Here's where the fun starts, cast your mind back to the time that you were courting, remember how you used to love those slow dances, pressing your intended tightly against you? Remember how you couldn't keep your hands to yourself? Remember how you used to park in some quiet spot and sit talking into the small hours? Remember? It may sound a little strange now, but the fact is that getting physical and sharing an honest conversation, are the best stress relief valves that there are, so start again.

I don't mean you should march straight in, throw your wife or hubby down on the shag-pile and get at it! Do that and you'll frighten the cat, or worse, the kids will take photos and blackmail you for extra pocket-money. You can be more gentle, a kind word and an embrace will do; believe me, it's worth the risk, and the pressure will be relieved so quickly, that NASA may well phone you.

A few minutes in the arms of your spouse or swarming about in a tangled heap of arms and legs with the kids will relieve all the stress that's going, which means that you'll live longer. And you will enjoy your family more, which means that it will be worth living longer.

To make this home-coming progress smoothly, I've laid down a few simple rules. But don't worry, they're my rules so they're really easy to remember, and they are uncannily similar to the rules used during any other sales presentation.

Rule one – open the sale
Open the sale, remember how we do that, a smile, a greeting. When you walk through your door, make sure you are looking your best; wearing your biggest smile, exuding that professional air of positivity and confidence; treat it like any other sales call, first a smile, then the greeting. You could just say "hello" and wait for the reply but, come on, you don't really need words; these are the folk that you love, greet them with a huge hug and if you're really feeling like a superstar, a kiss. Your greeting should tell them that there is at least one person in this hard old world that loves them. That person is you.

Rule two – develop rapport
Remember how we develop rapport, pay your partner a

compliment. After the hug, say something nice. I didn't say
that this was easy, just that they're easy rules. Sometimes the
doing part has you thinking quickly on your feet, but as
salespeople you're used to that: "Sweetheart, how considerate of you to remember that I like my meat well done.
The way you have created the charcoal taste of a summer
barbecue in our electric oven, must have taken a lot of
practice. Did you ask the fire brigade to fetch pussy down
from the tree while they were here?"

But seriously, the finest compliment to either husband or
wife, is to tell them how sexy they look, it can turn out being
the most fun one too!

Rule three

Before you tell husband about all the disasters that befell you
during your toils today, tell him the best thing that happened:
"Had a very interesting meeting with the boss, this morning.
He said that my recent sales figures had him simply
speechless." Home is a place to be secure in. Lock the
disasters out where the burglars lurk.

Rule four

Ask wife about her day, listen with interest to all she has to
say; you are possibly the first adult she has had to converse
with since breakfast, so give her a chance to relieve the
tensions in her own existence.

Rule five

The first do not. Never say to your children: "I'm too busy."
One of the noblest ambitions in life is to grow old enough to
become a nuisance to your own kids. Don't give them the
excuse to say to you: "Not today dad, I'm too busy." Besides,
the Psychologists tell us that our children choose to interpret
our words in ways which could well horrify us did we but
know. "I'm too busy," to a three-year-old may well sound
like: "Go away you have no right to exist in this house!"

Rule six

Perhaps the most important. Your home is the haven for your sanity so don't let customers into it. Never be tempted to tell your business contacts what your home phone number is. Most folk who phone you at home are calling to share something unpleasant with you. Make them wait until you are being paid for it before they swamp you in bad attitude.

It's becoming fashionable today to have a cellular installed in the car. Forget it. When you decide that you are going to invest a few hours in a family outing, to make up for a week of late nights and rainy weekends, the last thing you need is an embarrassing barrage of abuse pouring out of the dash board and the kids asking: "What exactly do those words mean daddy, only that's what teacher said I was, when I set fire to her desk yesterday?"

My rules end here. You have the opportunity when you pursue a career in selling, to achieve the level of success that you desire. Much more so than in any other walk of life. You will be guaranteed success if you ensure that that's the way it stays. Pursue success rather than letting success pursue you. The latter is a whole different outlook and one which is much more miserable in the achievement.

It's one thing taking your work seriously, but not that seriously that it takes over your life. Make the last call of the day your best call every day, and you can go to work each morning, just knowing that there is at least one call to look forward to. It's better than quitting sales for a job in an office or factory. The purple-faced fiend lives in those places as well. Only it isn't so easy to avoid him.

OUR PUBLISHING POLICY

HOW WE CHOOSE

Our policy is to consider every deserving manuscript and we can give special editorial help where an author is an authority on his subject but an inexperienced writer. We are rigorously selective in the choice of books we publish. We set the highest standards of editorial quality and accuracy. This means that a *Paperfront* is easy to understand and delightful to read. Where illustrations are necessary to convey points of detail, these are drawn up by a subject specialist artist from our panel.

HOW WE KEEP PRICES LOW

We aim for the big seller. This enables us to order enormous print runs and achieve the lowest price for you. Unfortunately, this means that you will not find in the *Paperfront* list any titles on obscure subjects of minority interest only. These could not be printed in large enough quantities to be sold for the low price at which we offer this series.

We sell almost all our *Paperfronts* at the same unit price. This saves a lot of fiddling about in our clerical departments and helps us to give you world-beating value. Under this system, the longer titles are offered at a price which we believe to be unmatched by any publisher in the world.

OUR DISTRIBUTION SYSTEM

Because of the competitive price, and the rapid turnover, *Paperfronts* are possibly the most profitable line a bookseller can handle. They are stocked by the best bookshops all over the world. It may be that your bookseller has run out of stock of a particular title. If so, he can order more from us at any time—we have a fine reputation for "same day" despatch, and we supply any order, however small (even a single copy), to any bookseller who has an account with us. We prefer you to buy from your bookseller, as this reminds him of the strong underlying public demand for *Paperfronts*. Members of the public who live in remote places, or who are housebound, or whose local bookseller is unco-operative, can order direct from us by post.

FREE

If you would like an up-to-date list of all Paperfront titles currently available, send a stamped self-addressed envelope to
ELLIOT RIGHT WAY BOOKS, BRIGHTON RD.,
LOWER KINGSWOOD, SURREY, U.K.